*How to*
# CHANGE YOUR LIFE
*in*
# 10
# MINUTES
## A DAY

*How to*

# CHANGE YOUR LIFE

*in*

# 10
# MINUTES
## A DAY

The Deep Dive into Applications
of the 10-Minute Philosophy

MICHAL STAWICKI
www.expandbeyondyourself.com

How to Change Your Life in 10  Minutes a day:
The Deep Dive into Applications
of the 10-Minute Philosophy

# Contents

# From Shy to Hi
Tame Social Anxiety, Meet New People
and Build Self-Confidence

How to **Change Your Life** in **10 Minutes** a Day

# 10 Minutes

I'm deeply convinced that daily, consistent action absolutely must lead to results. Period. Well, to say that "I'm convinced" is putting it mildly. **I KNOW that daily, sustained action brings results.**

I know it because I do practice this rule in many areas of my life. I focus daily on specific actions, committing 10minutes to them. I do track my results. And I do see them improving. I got results in such different areas as weight loss, finances, learning skills and relationships. I strongly suppose that it is a universal law applicable to absolutely ALL areas of life.

If you do something daily and you are not getting the desired results, it simply means you are putting at least as much daily and sustainable effort against those results.

Let me give you a practical example. If you exercise 10 minutes a day, the same routine day by day by day, your muscles have to become stronger and your weight must drop, UNLESS, you counteract your exercises by introducing more calories to your diet, or by lying on the couch for the rest of the day.

The more action, the better results, up to some reasonable level - take a look at this chart:

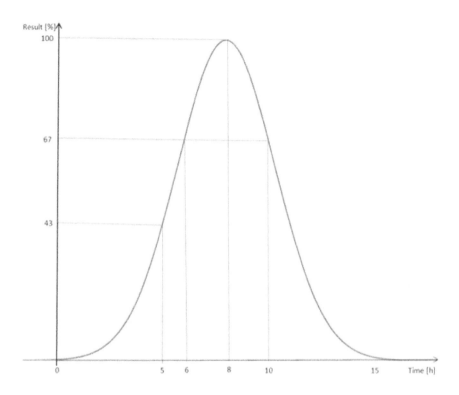

The shape of the curve is called normal distribution in probability research. It is in statistics something like the number $\pi$ in math. As $\pi$ can be found in many equations describing the texture of the universe, normal distribution can be used to describe a multitude of quantities in physics and measurements in biology, including IQ, height, weight and many more.

According to central limit theorem, the mean of a large number of random variables tends to normal distribution. And in our big and complicated world, a lot of effects are presented by a large number of random data. I did study the statistics (years ago) and still don't understand most of this stuff, and it's out of the scope of this book, anyway. If you are curious, it is explained in a forthright way here:

http://askville.amazon.com/Central-Limit-THeorem-apply-statistics-life/AnswerViewer.do?requestId=7620607

To drive a point home (and to get away from scientific theories) please compare my pictures (below and on page 4) with the photos of my friend on page 5:

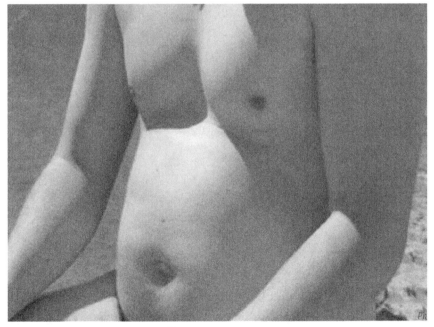

Summer 2011

I lost about 25 lbs. in 10 months.

Nathan lost over 40 lbs. within 90 days. I used about 25 minutes a day for my overall fitness program, his daily walk to a grocery store - and it was just a small part of his program - took him more than 30 minutes every day.

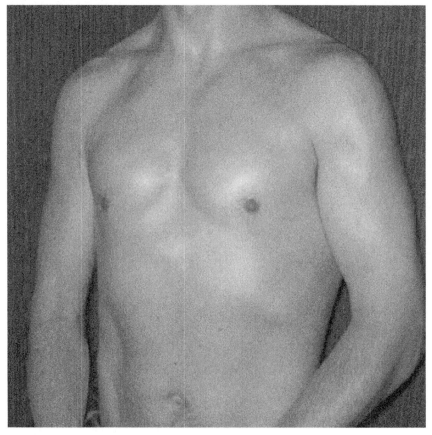

May 2013

I believe the normal distribution can be also applied to describe a relation between a human effort represented by time and achieved results.

We have to sleep, so we have about 16 hours at our disposal and we can get the maximum result investing half of them in one activity. If we give less time, we don't achieve the maximum result, and if we dedicate too much time, we are burning out.

But we are not going to devote 8 hours a day of our precious life to get the maximum result, which in this case would be ... a world bodybuilding championship, I suppose.

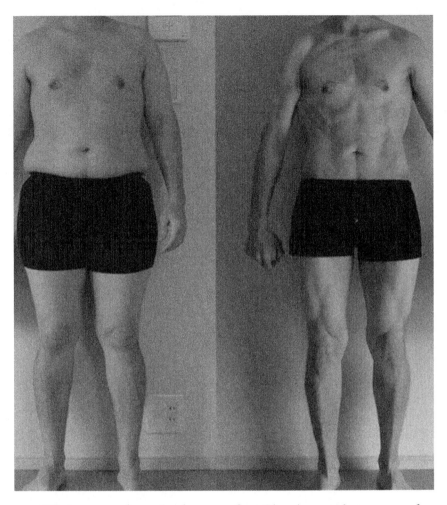

We just need to shed some fat. Check out the zoomed left part of the first chart:

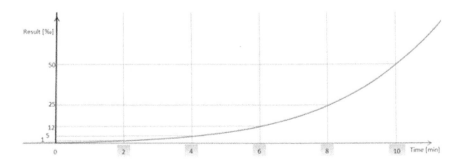

I used the weight loss example, but it applies to absolutely everything in life. I tested this concept in building relationships, learning new skills (e.g. speed reading), spiritual life, writing, overcoming shyness, time management, and many more. It always works.

Even the smallest amount of invested time brings results. I consciously use about 2 minutes of my day on savings and I do a few monthly activities - a budget summary, paying bills, dividing my resources between different assets and so on - it takes me about 2 hours, so overall, it's 6 minutes a day. And it brings me the results.

Quite recently, I met a guy who learned to play guitar practicing just 7 minutes a day. He has been doing it for three years and he is much better than me, although I have been playing a guitar for about 10 years. I just don't practice playing a guitar daily. My action is not sustained, so his results are more impressive.

Ten minutes is just a handy number. It can be two minutes and you still get the results. They'll just be microscopic and take around 50 times as long to see than if you had spent 10 minutes instead.

There are only two 100% effective methods to not achieve any goal: never start or give up (before you reach it).

But every - even the tiniest - consistent action brings result.

It's the core of this philosophy and it overcomes the two major obstacles of any lasting change: fear of failure, which stops us even before we begin, and giving up, which stops us after we begin, but before we get things done.

**Every** action brings results in the end. As long as you do something, you can't fail. There is no failure. You have nothing to fear. You can begin without the burden of hesitations and doubts.

And giving up is out of the question. What can cause you to resign, if you **know** that the results are inevitable, that all you need is just to sustain your action?

Giving up is not like an early withdrawal, where you get your money back, and sometimes even a part of the interest. It's like being in an investment program. Your obligation is to invest $1,000 every month, and if you do it for 5 years, you will get your $60,000 of capital and guaranteed $40,000 of the return on the investment. However, if you break the agreement you will get only part of your capital - from 10% in the first year of a contract to 50% in the last year - and none of the returns.

I'm fond of this simile, as it's not only about the process of getting results, but also, what you are going to do when you achieve them. After 5 years, you can decide on what to do with your money. You can put all of it back into the investment program again, or you can just spend everything. It's the same with any change in your life; it's the same with a weight loss. You can make yourself fit and then go back to your unhealthy habits and lose everything you've been doing for the last several months or years. Or you can build on it, for example by writing a Kindle booklet about a weight loss ;)

*"All right"* - you say - *"but those are some fancy stories and theories. How is it applicable in my life?"*

I concur – theorization alone is quite useless. What caused me to embrace this philosophy wasn't other's stories and preaching. It was my own stories.

In order to feel at a gut level that it is indeed a universal law, applicable also to you, please give a thought to any successful area of your life. It can be anything - your marriage, a specific skill, a career, the fact that you have never had a car accident, good grades at school, a patience, your great relationship with your parents. The best thing for this little exercise is something you take for granted, but other people are praising you for. So, pick one and think: what makes you successful in this area? What's the difference between you and people who praise you, who aren't so successful? What do you do that they don't?

I bet you will find some consistent action underlying your success.

I take the love in my family for granted. I hadn't noticed it until my newfound online friends drew my attention to it by their comments on my personal blog. I have given it some thought and discovered that I say "I love you" to my wife and kids every day. When I was a teenager, I realized that, in my family, those words were ... well, maybe not a taboo, but close to it. I didn't hear those words very often at my home. And I was missing it. So I decided in my heart, that when I start **my** family, I will say this to **my** family members as often as I feel like it. It happened to be every day. In fact, several times each day. And this simple action makes all the difference in our family life.

And it's just one instance of this law. I have found many other examples behind my big and small successes - the high-school diploma, the scholarship on the 4th year of university studies, my personal fitness records.

It is true. You will find such examples in your life, too.

Look at the time/results chart once again. You probably noticed how the results grow exponentially after some point. As I said earlier - the more time you invest, the better results you get. I'm just assuming that weight-loss is not your first priority, so you don't want to invest much time. I understand you have your family to take care of, bills to pay, work to do, people to help, projects to attend to, relationships to keep or improve. A weight-loss comes after all of those activities in your life, so it's natural some additional pounds on your body have been developed. You have more pressing matters to take care of. You only have 24 hours and it's hard to find time for anything else. Thus, 10 minutes.

## Philosophical Points to Remember

- every sustained action brings a result
- the keyword is "sustained," don't give up
- sustained action in the opposite direction will neutralize your good deeds
- find examples of the above truths in your life to embrace this philosophy on a personal level

# THE
# FITNESS EXPERT
# NEXT DOOR

## How to Set and Reach
## Realistic Fitness Goals
## in 10 Minutes a Day

# Introduction

I am not a fitness guru; not even a personal trainer. I'm not a diet specialist. On the other hand, while not being any of the above, I did manage to lose 15 percent of my body weight (I'm a short and skinny guy; in absolute numbers, it is just 25 pounds). I can do 100 consecutive pushups, 54 consecutive dips, 33 consecutive chin-ups. And I didn't need any fitness guru, personal trainer, gym membership or diet consultant to do this. I didn't spend a lot of time or a lot of money. Weight-loss is just a by-product of my life's transition. And my fitness form is just a by-product of my weight loss.

I'm a busy person – a full-time employee (I spend about 18 hours a week commuting), father of three and a husband, a church community member, a blogger. But I discovered I don't need a lot of time (in daily terms) or money to lose weight. By sharing my story and advice, I want to convince you that you don't, either.

I intended this book to show purely my personal story, but then I ran across an old friend of mine that I hadn't seen in 10 years. He is also a busy father, husband and employee. And he lost about 12-percent bodyweight on his own. It made me think that my story is not so unique.

Well, it is, of course, because every human being is unique; nonetheless, there are lots and lots of ordinary people's stories about getting fitter – people who changed their lives for the better.

I was already writing this book when I stumbled upon research published last year in the American Journal of Preventive Medicine showing exactly that. They surveyed over 4,000 obese people (BMI >29.9), among whom over 2,500 reported an attempt to lose weight. Over 1,500 got significant results. Research showed also that simple strategies were a greater success factor than participating in a commercial weight-loss program.

Over 60 percent of fatties who attempted to lose weight got significant results!

Weight-loss is not rocket science. It's not something reserved for the privileged, movie stars and TV presenters. Ordinary folks burdened with duties, jobs and families can do it, too. Thousands of people like you and me do it every year, every month, every day. Your neighbor did it. You can do it, too.

Les Brown said: "You will fail your way to success."

And he is so right! I failed my way to weight loss. I had vague thoughts about losing some weight as long as 5.5 years ago. I started seriously losing some pounds a year ago. 54 months of failure! I did everything backwards. I started from the totally wrong point and gradually drifted in the right direction. And I found tactics which bring results.

I'm not going to impose my super-effective fitness program on you and charge $39 for it.

You don't need my knowledge to lose weight. Not that it is insufficient; it allowed me to get my results. The knowledge is at your fingertips – the Internet is full of diets, workouts and fitness programs. They work for some people; for other people, they don't. I don't accuse the fitness industry of preying on the naivety of their prospects. All those different programs have their advantages and are effective – under specific conditions. If you do what they say, when they say and in the way they say, you (usually) get the results. But the problem is, you must bend to those rules, and there is no universal detailed method which will work for everyone.

Imposing my rules on you will not be necessarily effective, anyway. For example, my wife decided to lose some weight when she noticed she was several pounds heavier than me. She asked me for advice. I answered, "Eat carrots as a snack," because that was what worked for me. She did it and got a stomach pain. I didn't even propose she follow the murderous workout program I practice, due to one simple reason – she hates physical exercises. From all the physical activities, the one she enjoys most is shopping. To be specific – shopping for outfits.

What you need is an incentive. An internal motivation. A story which will make you think that this is actually doable in your case, too. A few simple tips that will point you in the right direction. A fundament of "10 minutes philosophy," which you can make your very own life philosophy. This book is intended to help you to come up with your strategy – one that will work for you, so you can decide on your conditions, your time frames, your methods and your results. And above all, that will be believable for you, so you actually will start, will take action, based on this strategy.

# Psychology

If you are a hardcore realist, feel free to skip this chapter. Just read the bullet points at the end. Remember however, that I've been there, done that. And I claim that your mindset is 80% of your weight loss.

## Misconceptions about Weight Loss

I think there are a lot of false and sometimes even conflicting concepts about changing one's life, including, but not limited to:

- you need to have a monstrous will power
- you need a specific talent
- you need tremendous perseverance
- you need luck
- you need to work really hard to succeed
- you need to sacrifice a lot of time to get the results
- you need to get results fast or you will lose momentum and give up
- you need a big, challenging goal

Weight-loss is an area where all of these myths are really affecting people's minds. Don't get me wrong - all of the above points can be very handy in weight loss, but they are not critical. It's not that if you don't have luck or will power or a lot of time, then you can't lose weight.

## A Reason to Change

What amazes me is that the key factor to any lasting change is so often overlooked: you need a compelling reason to change. I pinpointed a formula for any transformation:

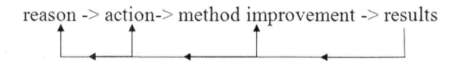

Each of the links in this "chain of change" is necessary. For example, without improving your method, you won't get good enough results to help you continue with your weight-loss program. Seeing that it doesn't work the way you wanted, you will just give up. Each one is also hooked up to the feedback loop.

Not a single component of this formula needs to be perfect, brilliant or impressive. It's enough that it leads to another step of the cycle. So the only thing you need at the beginning is a reason, which will make you to take action.

Everyone needs his or her own reason. My appearance wasn't a good enough motivator for me. I was getting rounder and rounder, but that didn't make me want to do anything about my weight. However, a little discomfort was enough to put me into action mode.

When I was 16 years old, I injured my spine jumping into a swimming pool. It was nothing serious, but when

I got fatter, my strained spine began to hurt. The pain was annoying, coming back again and again in the least expected moments. And it was the reason I started my more than 5 year long quest for a weight loss. A friend of mine, who has already lost 37 lbs. and is on a quest to lose more, has a very similar reason: sedentary job, back pain. But my wife's reason was: "my husband can't weigh less than me!"

And I know you have your own, unique reason. If not, you wouldn't be reading this book.

## The Snowball Effect

At the beginning, your expectations are not big, especially when you start with a firm decision to commit only 10 minutes a day. You just want to get rid of some fat from your body. So you start by developing a mundane habit like eating raw carrots as a snack. Then you start noticing changes and the snowball effect kicks in.

You can't even imagine what this small, insignificant discipline will bring to you. I just wanted to be thinner and pain-free. I got that and much more:

- I have a big Adam's apple. I felt strangled buttoning up my shirt collars. If I wanted to feel comfortable, I was forced to wear shirts one size bigger. But I lost fat from my neck and I can button up collars on all of my shirts. Neck fat! I would never have believed there was such a thing.

- my self-image skyrocketed. It's not that I had troubles with my self-image before. Why should I? I was just 8 lbs. above the 'normal' BMI boundary. I considered myself immune to such low opinions, the way I look does not determine my worth! I was wrong. I could be immune to the shallow judgments regarding obese people, but it came out that I'm not immune to those regarding muscular ones. I'm the same person inside, but I like myself more looking in the mirror and seeing a tough, muscular guy.

- my wife started her own weight-loss program, because "my husband cannot weigh less than me" ;) Now she enjoys all the additional blessings of weight loss, too.

- I can run without much effort. I'm not a runner type. To give you the picture - my 10-year-old son is almost as fast as me (but he is the fastest among 10-year-old boys in his school). Yet, I need to jog quite often to catch a bus or a train, about twice a week. I used to feel exhausted; after each "race to the train," I was literally half-dead and out of breath. And now running feels terrific.

- the social acceptance of my transition is a great boost to my self-confidence. My friends and family are telling me they admire me, my efforts, my new look. As an adult human being, I shouldn't care much about other's opinions, but I do. Shame on me ;)

- I regularly beat my own fitness records - number of consecutive pull ups, pushups, dips. I like competing against myself. I like getting better results. I like my life more.

- my muscles showed up. I trained rigorously for years, but all my muscles were hidden under the layer of fat.

That all is happening because I wanted to get rid of back pain. The reward is always bigger than you can imagine at the start.

## You Are What You Think About

Embracing this simple truth will help you enormously in your weight loss. It's not just some hocus-pocus twaddle. Yes, I know you need to change your lifestyle, eating habits, introduce exercises. But those are secondary things. It's not 'going mystical.' It is about results.

I'm one of the most businesslike persons on this planet and that's why I'm putting a mind before a body. I know what I'm talking about. I got the best results not by a strict diet or an exhaustive training, but by applying a simple mental exercise which helped my mind to focus on the adequate physical means.

I'm not saying that you'll lose your fat just by a hefty dose of daydreaming - absolutely not! The fat will not magically disappear, because you will cast a spell on it by the power of your mind. The physical means are necessary, they are just less effective alone or being put in the first place, before thinking.

I don't want you to become a master of your thoughts. Well, I do, but I'm not a master of my thoughts, so I'm not entitled to teach on that subject. I believe that conquering your mind and self-talk is a task much more intensive than losing some weight, and it's out of the scope of this book. You may be a god of a tiny part of the universe which consists solely of yourself. You can control it perfectly.

However, this book is not intended to make you a Zen master, who controls himself absolutely, but to make you to start or enhance your weight-loss program. And to do it fast and relatively easy. I'm quite serious about "10 minutes" in the book's title.

I will not encourage you to say to yourself a hundred times a day: "I'm fit, healthy and fabulous," when you can clearly see your rolls of fat in the mirror. But you have to be conscious that your self-talk, this immaterial process taking part inside your head, does affect your outer world. Thinking: "I'm fat, I'm hopeless, I'm fat," a hundred times a day is not going to help you, either. Such thoughts are the shortest way to failure. How long, do you think, will you persevere in your commitment (even a 10-minute commitment) while being bombarded by those kinds of messages from the inside?

The right thinking is important. I've never doubted I can lose weight. Maybe it's because in my mind's eye, I had the skinny pictures of me from my adolescence. That's more or less what "The Secret's" gurus say. Anyway, I had no doubts, so weight-loss seemed so easy to me. Persevering in my efforts for four years without visible results wasn't a problem for me.

Of course, you are a unique being and you can't borrow my mind set. It is just an example illustrating a victory of mind over matter. Looking from the outside, I was a hopeless failure. But my inner attitude got me through this experience to the point of getting some results. Don't dismiss the power of mind. Do not diminish it.

If you think in a wrong way, you won't even begin to take action.

## Psychological Points to Remember

- you need a good reason for wanting to change
- your reason must ignite you to start an action
- you are not an animal; your thoughts do determine your actions
- your reason (and rewards) will grow with your weight loss progress

# You Are What You Do

The thinking takes place before action, but it is action which brings results. You need right thinking or good enough thinking in the first place, so you'll take action, persevere and not give up. And that is 80% of success. The last 20% is proper action, skills and knowledge.

80% of action should be directed at the critical activities - more about that later. And it should be done in the right direction and steadily. As I explained before - you can't commit 10 minutes to your weight loss, then 30 minutes against it, and expect a positive net result. In other words - if you act that way, then what you do determines who you are. And you are not a weight loser anymore - you are a weight gainer.

## Start Right Now

No amount of thinking will substitute for action. A few hours of thinking plus a few minutes of acting may do for the multitude. Months of thinking or dreaming without taking action is wasted time.

Going from the world of mind to the world of matter,

from plan to action, is simple.

Just do it.

Take action.

Start today.

After each chapter, there are some bullet points. Pick one and practice it today.

Go and search for info. Do a set of pushups. Plan your diet. Schedule time for exercise. Buy different kinds of veggies to discover your tastes. Register on a weight-loss forum. Do something. Anything. Start gaining momentum.

There is no wrong way to start.

## Persevere

Perseverance and consistency are necessary to achieve any results, at least in my world. I'm not talking here about quick fixes, winning the lottery, an extraordinary business proposal which will change your life without any initial investment and much work.

Get real. Be realistic. Get rid of marketing cataracts from your mind's eyes. Movie stars and politics don't really look as perfect as on TV. Heck! Most fitness gurus look at least a little worse in person than on their training videos. The Internet is full of 'get-rich-quick' schemes: "gimme your money and I'll show you how to get rich in no time!" Well, the disclaimers are there, too, of course. Put at the bottom of the page in fine print.

Our minds are bombarded by those kinds of messages all the time. And we are what we think about. We are all in a "get fit, rich, beautiful, happy and get it quickly" mindset. There are notable exceptions, but they are few and far between. Think of it. How many people do you know who exercise daily for at least one year? How many people who attend their church at least once a week for ten years or more? How many people who have a financial surplus? Compare those numbers to the number of people you know who visit Facebook every day, who watch TV every day, who eat sweets or chips every day.

We choose to satisfy our desires with quick and easy pleasures, instead of satisfying our needs by a sustained effort.

Behind 99% of success, there is certain to be hidden years of hard work, experience, blood, sweat and tears.

I know a story of a dentist who became a very successful Internet marketer. He sells the blueprint for other dentists on how to establish a profitable dental assistant school. Within 14 months, he sold this blueprint to over 50 locations. There were just 300 names on his list when he made his first launch and he made $140,000. The second launch to the list of almost 700 brought him another $90,000. Can you imagine what a clever marketer could do with such a story? I can see those imaginary headlines: "Make over $128 to $450 per your list member!" "Financial success in 14 months!"

And a fine print disclaimer at the bottom of the page: "We cannot guarantee anything, but you can achieve best results if you are a dentist (at least seven years of study!), start your own practice, start a dental assistant school working your butt off in the evenings after your practice for several years and then structure, systematize, market and sell a blueprint for such a school program."

Doesn't sound so inviting anymore, huh? But a dentist I'm talking about did exactly that. He worked 12 years to get to a point where he monetized his hard work. His first attempt to sell a blueprint through the Internet was unsuccessful - he sold just two products within a year. How would he be if he gave up the idea then? Well, $230,000 worse off.

You and I both know that this is the way to get the things done in the real world. Begin, work continuously, work hard, work smart, work as long as it takes to get the results. And there is no "give up" in this formula.

No matter if you invest 10 minutes a day or 10 years of your life into some venture - giving up will have exactly the same effect - null, nada, zero, zilch.

As long as you continue your commitment, there is a chance to succeed. The moment you stop is the moment this chance is lost. Never give up.

There are several reasons we usually give up, and the 10-minute philosophy can help you to beat up all of them.

- we give up because the task seems to be big and scary, just too hard to do. Well, in this instance, it's just 10 minutes, how hard could it be?

- we give up because it looks like achieving the result will just take forever (well, it's only several weeks or months, but we live in the Internet, impatient era, we want it yesterday). But it will not take forever. It will take 10 minutes and your result (for today) will be achieved.

- we give up because our motivation drained. And it's much, much easier to motivate yourself for a 10-minute task than it is to lose 15% of your bodyweight in the next 10 months.

All in all, perseverance connotes with a long, hard, monumental job to do, and a mere 10 minutes is no such thing, is it? It's trivial.

OK, a photo to illustrate the point (one picture is worth

more than a thousand words):

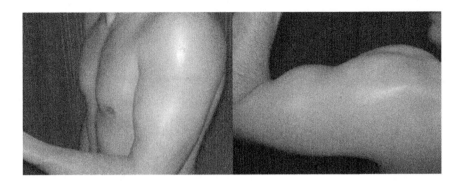

Those muscles were built by the thousands and thousands and thousands of pushups. I had been doing them when I was a fatty. They weren't done in one moment, day, week, month or even a whole year. It was several years. What is more, until quite recently, I did just one single consecutive series of pushups a day, which took me just 2-8 minutes. I would never have seen those muscles if I had given up doing pushups before losing my layer of fat.

## Be Creative

We've covered the critical parts of taking action - firstly start, then never give up. However, which action you take is also pivotal. Don't get yourself locked into a certain kind of acting, which doesn't bring you results. It's not enough to be positive in your thinking and to take continuous action. Those elements are necessary, but if your actions drive you in the wrong direction, no amount of activity will achieve your weight-loss goal.

Let's compare weight loss to a voyage. It's not enough to define the destination, start the engine and move forward - you must drive in the right direction to reach your goal.

If you took a wrong turn, being persistent will do you no good. You must make a U-turn, drive back and correct your route.

Be flexible with your approach.

You know best what's good for you. You know your circumstances, attitudes and fancies. And you are the best person in the world to compose your weight-loss program. If you like physical exercises, you can find an appropriate training on the market and use it, not the other way around: to buy a training and then make yourself do it against your predispositions.

It might happen, that once you commit to your weight-loss activities and do them for an extended period of time, you will find that you enjoy them or enjoy the results to such an extent that you are actually willing to put more of your resources into your program, more time or more money. But that's for the future. I was willing to give more only after three years. But being 'cheap' about my program did wonders for my creativity. I give you some examples to enhance yours:

**1.** I'm a fan of short, intensive exercises. I mean really short and really intensive. Usually, I do a consecutive series of one routine to the point I can't do even one more repetition.

I started doing pushups regularly 5.5 years ago. For the first two years, this simple exercise was enough for me. I did one consecutive series - as many pushups as I could. I started from about 40 and reached about 130. But man (oops! sorry gals), that took time! And I don't mean, it took me 2 or 3 years to reach 130 consecutive pushups level, but it took me about 7-8 minutes to finish the exercise. So I started to introduce changes to my routine - first, it was narrow-grip pushups, then diamond pushups, then all of the above with legs elevated. All of them were harder to do than normal pushups, so the time of my 'training window' stopped growing and even shrank a little.

I was doing over 80 legs-elevated pushups when I got the idea to put my kids on my back. Jackpot! My trainings started to be shorter and more intensive at the same time.

Unfortunately, I wake up for the morning shift about 5 a.m., and my children are not available so early. What is more, my wife complained that my exercises are too loud, my gasping for air wakes her up. Instead of giving up my work outs, I came up with a different idea. Being on the morning shift, I started to do dips instead of pushups.

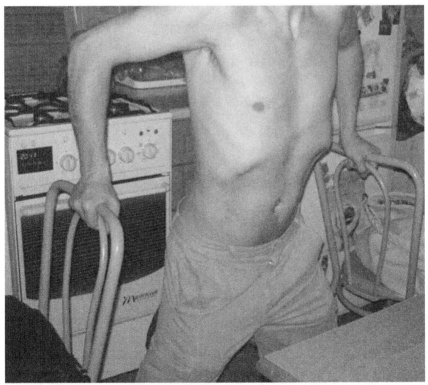

**Do-it-yourself creativity example: chairs dips**

At the beginning, I was able to do about 20 consecutive dips. Again, it was faster and I made less noise. I used (and still use) my kitchen chairs as bars.

**2.** About 2 to 2.5 years ago, I bought a bar for pull ups, the cheapest stuff from the supermarket (less than $10). And it stayed hidden behind the bed for six months, because I had no drill to install it with.

At last, my mate, who is a carpenter, installed it when he was fixing some furniture in my apartment. Pull-ups are just great, they are the shortest workout I can imagine doing using only my body weight.

In the beginning, I did just 14 chin-ups.

**3.** When I came to a doctor with my spine problem, she advised me to work on my belly muscles. I got fired up with excitement dreaming about sexy abs.

But what to do? Sit-ups? I did 100 and felt I could do more! It appeared that pushups are great for belly muscles, too. So I found another body weight exercise - Weider series - and started to use it. Right, my belly muscles were strained, but soon the exercise took more and more of my time. And I didn't have the time. So I created it. I set an alarm clock 15 minutes earlier. I had already been waking up terribly early - about 5 a.m. - and 15 minutes made little difference. Unfortunately, I discovered that having sexy abs is hard to accomplish with just a quarter of a body-weight exercise.

**4.** I'm the one with a sweet tooth. Maybe even THE one. I could easily eat two pounds of cake in one afternoon. I love sweets. I'm an addict. When I realized I need to change my diet, it was quite easy to target my vice. But what to do with that? I've come up with an idea to at least partially replace sweets with raw carrots.

Why carrots? They are cheap, available all year long and I like them. Whenever I had an urge to eat something full of sugar, I took a carrot instead. That was the first trigger allowing me to shed several pounds.

**5**. Then, I realized I don't know much about healthy eating and diets. Up to that point, it was "a woman's thing" for me. I did some research on the Internet. Under the layer of mystical spells I found the bottom line - calorie intake. I found a great website where I can check almost every scrap of food for the number of calories. I paid attention to what I eat. I composed a reasonable daily diet from the foods I eat and like. I reduced the amount of bread I ate by about 25%. You might ask: what's so creative about that? Well, I made my own plan of meals. I didn't choose any specific diet, imposed from the outside. And because it was mine, I stuck to it.

**6**. You need to be committed over a long period of time to get results, especially if your energy or effort input is low.

I was still looking for any additional methods or tools I could use, as I still wasn't satisfied with the output.

I don't remember where I got the idea of a food journal, or as I call it - a diet log. For sure it was not mine. Anyway, I started to keep it on the 3rd of January 2013. It's a very simple tactic and from the rational perspective, it shouldn't make any difference at all. I didn't burn many calories writing on a computer's keyboard for three minutes a day, I didn't change my workout regime or diet. However, it made all the difference. I've achieved my dream weight two months and six days later.

## Action Points to Remember

- start right now!
- persevere
- monitor your methods and progress; adjust them, if necessary
- be creative

# Two Dark Secrets

There are just two very secret rules of weight loss hidden in safe deposits of fitness gurus, so we common mortals cannot reach them and be fit. I will reveal them right now and revolutionize your life forever. Those rules are:

- eat less
- move more

The more important one is "eat less." If you are not anorexic or bulimic, bending to this rule will give you the best results.

Eat less

If you take just one piece of data from this book, this one is the most important in weight loss: **Proper eating is 80% of your weight-loss success**. Your eating habits, your foods intake, determines the output of your fat-loss efforts. "Eat less" is a magic formula for losing weight, if you look for one. There is no other.

The prevailing strategy (65% responses) among respondents of the research I mentioned at the beginning of this book was: eat less. The research showed also that it was more efficient than participating in a commercial weight-loss program.

Weight-loss can be reduced to a simple math formula – it is all about the number of calories you eat and burn. There is more to it of course - your body assimilates different types of food at a different pace, your digestive system works more efficiently at specific times of day, physical exercises can boost your metabolism, and so on. However, the bottom line is to maintain the calorie-deficit, and it can be represented by a formula:

**calories eaten - calories burned = weight loss**

But what really makes this formula less practical is an unpredictable human behavior. For example, the advice not to eat late in the evening has to do less with our metabolism and more with our attitudes. Yes, your body works slower while you sleep, but it doesn't mean your supper will be mysteriously transformed into fat tissue. Your body just needs more time to digest it. What is really dangerous in late eating is the types of food we usually consume then: junk food, snacks, sweets, alcohol.

Thus, the weight-loss researchers could easily connote night-eating with obesity, and conclude the finding that one leads to the other.

I've told you before about my friend who lost 37 lbs. I asked him: "What method have you used?" He answered: "The scientific method. I ate less calories than my body used." And because he believed that, he could dismiss all the contradicting philosophies - eat this, don't eat that; eat six small meals, no, eat just two and apply intermittent fasting; eat fruits on an empty stomach, no, use them as snacks - and focus on the bottom line, which is calorie intake. I'm not saying some of them are not valid or at least valid in specific circumstances, but they are just minor details in your weight loss. It doesn't matter what you eat or when you eat, if you eat too much!

So, use the "scientific method" of my friend. Focus on how much you eat, know your daily calorie intake. That's your grand strategy. Types of meals, time of meals and their frequency are mere tactical means.

I can easily read your mind right now: "But what do you mean eat less? Are you advising me to starve? I eat just enough to function normally, I'm not overeating!"

Well, you think you are not overeating. Exactly as I thought before my weight loss quest. I'll tell you this: If your BMI result is above 26, then you are overeating. Take a look at my fat photo at the beginning of the book. The man you see there is not obese. I was just a little overweight - just several pounds. And I was overeating.

Five years ago, I used to eat four double sandwiches of white bread at work:

I also ate a breakfast and a late lunch at home. And a doughnut about every 2-3 days. And a cake every time there was an occasion to eat one. And some sweets in the evenings. Compare the amount of food I then ate with my today's diet:

- 3 slices of whole grain bread with ham. A big cup of tea with one spoon of sugar and rum
- 2 chops of chuck with potatoes and onion
- 4 chips
- 2 jellybeans
- one orange
- one carrot
- 4 slices of whole grain bread with honey. A big cup of chicory coffee with milk

So, I ate less and I survived. Well, I thrive, in fact. I have never felt better physically in my life. I can comfortably wear my wedding suit (I've been married for almost 13 years). I'm beating my fitness records like crazy - about a dozen since January; four while writing this booklet. I've beaten the last one on the 2nd of July - 29 consecutive pull-ups. I'm in better shape than I was 15 years ago.

If you are anything like me from the photo, or bigger, there is still leeway. Thoughts of starvation is just a whining of your subconscious mind, which is trying to protect you against any changes. The primal fear of hunger is rooted deep inside us, but let's face it - it's not the hunger which is a safety hazard to our life today, it's an overconsumption.

You can eat less. It's possible. You must eat less in order to lose weight. If you still have a problem with that thought, if you still feel restricted, let me tell you a story which will put some light on this subject.

Some time ago, I think it was November 2012, I watched a TV program about obese people losing weight (my wife enjoys watching such shows on "the woman's" channel). Most of them did that by stomach stapling. But there was one guy who lost 400 pounds without any surgery or pharmacology. He told his philosophy of weight loss: "Eating is my addiction. I think it is the worst addiction of all, as eating itself is necessary to support my body with energy. I cannot break up with it, like with drugs or alcohol." He overcame his urges in the simplest possible way - he has only the food for his nearest meal at home. After a breakfast, he goes to the grocery to buy his lunch. After a lunch, he goes there again to buy his supper.

By the way, this is the same tactic Nathan (my friend from pictures in the first chapter) used to achieve rapid results in his weight-loss. He goes to the grocery every day to buy the food products only for the next day, too.

I sympathize with the TV show guy's philosophy. That kind of attitude to eating, especially to consuming sweets helped me enormously in my weight-loss. I'm a lifelong, irredeemable, sweets addict. I needed to recognize that truth to take measures against it. You, too, need to recognize the truth about your bad eating habits before fixing them.

Please do understand the moral of the story properly. Overly stressing out about what, how and how much you eat can be disastrous to your health, too. We all know the stories of anorexic or bulimic media celebrities, don't we? Jim Rohn in "Cultivating an Unshakeable Character" instanced a long-term Finnish research comparing the health of two groups of people. Members of the first group could eat what they wanted. The second group was closely supervised – they could eat only healthy foods and in specific quantities. The stress related to tracking and controlling their eating caused more damage to their health than a "free" diet to the health of the first group's members.

Every extremity is dangerous. But most of our society, me two years ago and probably you reading this book, are just on the other side of extreme. We are absolutely careless about what and how much we eat. We don't think about it at all. To the effect, we eat too much. And that's the reason for our fat rolls.

Eating less is not a whim, it's the absolute bottom line of weight loss. **If you still feel rebellious about it, your first task is to overcome this feeling**. You will waste your time and energy attempting to lose weight with such an attitude. Don't buy a gym membership, don't look for magic pills or diets, don't start regular workouts - it all will be in vain, if you won't eat less.

Go and find your philosophy, the kind of thinking which will make you accept that eating less is not depriving you of life's pleasures, but giving you the lifestyle you want. The new, healthy and fit you. Find your deep reason. As I said in Chapter 3, it doesn't have to be big, just big enough to change your attitude and ignite you to start taking action. For my wife, the motivation is her conviction, that her husband shouldn't weigh less than her. Sensible? Not necessarily. "Good enough" to start an action? In her case: yes.

So, eat-less rebel (if you are one) - if you want to lose weight, the best way to start is investing your 10 minutes in the search for your philosophy. Keep looking until you find something stimulating you toward eating less. You don't have to become a fanatic of fasting. You just need to be comfortable with the fact that consuming less food is actually serving your purposes.

OK, enough is enough. We talked about "10 minute philosophy," about mind set, about the upmost importance of eating less in weight loss. Now, it's time to show you a technique which will both take you less than 10 minutes of your time, and bring big results. I did everything backwards and I want you to get much better results by doing things in the proper order. This is the first and foremost tool you should use. It is efficient even when you use it as a last resort, as I did, but why wait? Start out with it and you will see the change on the scale much faster than me.

## Keep a Diet Log

An incentive may be the first thing, but actual diet regime is important, too. If you didn't pay attention to your eating habits at all, you might have no idea as to what to cut out from your menu.

So it's time to introduce you to a diet log.

It's nothing innovative. It's known under many names: a food journal, a diet diary - just to name a couple. You use this simple technique by writing down everything that you eat and drink which contains calories. Every scrap of bread, every cookie, every glass of soda - everything. It is simple. It is mundane. It works.

Take it seriously. Make a plan how to go about it. Analyze your day, your eating patterns and decide on your tactic. You don't need an elaborate scheme or refined technical means. Keep it simple. Use a pen and a pocket notepad, iPad, a mobile phone - whatever suits you. It must be something you feel comfortable with and is easily accessible most of the time.

I spend more than a half of my life in front of a computer, so I found it congruent to log my food intake in a text file. If I was without computer access, I jotted down what I put into my mouth on a piece of paper, and later on typed it into a diet log file.

Take a look at a weekly excerpt from my log: http://www.expandbeyondyourself.com/dietlog/ That week, I lost a little more than one pound.

There are diet logs and diet logs. Some people write down a time of meal, the exact number of calories and how much water they've had. I just jotted down the amount and type of food and drink. I found it a "good enough" solution, as I wasn't supervising the Olympic Master fitness program, but an ordinary (and busy) man's weight-loss program. The main reason for keeping a diet log is to be aware of what and how much you eat. Being mindful makes miraculous changes to your behavior. Calculating the exact number of calories you consumed may be an additional feature, but one you need to put additional effort (and time) for.

Do treat keeping a diet log as a test of your real intentions. If you don't do it, you don't really want to lose weight; you are just playing with a thought to do it.

I mean, here I am - an expert. At least from your point of view, I'm assuming you are a reader who wants to lose weight – and I've already done it. I've managed to shave off fat, build some muscles and I've stuck with those changes. What is more, I did it with only marginal external guidance and by investing a minimal amount of time and resources. I made many mistakes along the way and I want you to avoid them, to choose the optimal path. And I'm telling you to do the simplest thing anyone is capable of doing. I insist it is important.

So, if you are not going to do it, what is that saying about your attitude? Are you really serious about your commitment?

You may come up with some reservations about a diet log, but you know what they really are? Excuses. Get serious. Get the job done. I'll help you by shooting down some excuses:

- I don't have time.

OK, I know. That's why I asked you to keep a diet log. It's the fastest, easiest and most efficient method to lose weight. You must be crippled or eat every 30 minutes to spend more than 10 minutes daily on your diet log.

- It's a lot of trouble.

Really? How? Carrying a pen and notepad is trouble for you?

- It is stupid hocus-pocus. No one lost even an ounce of fat by writing down things on paper!

I did. What is more, a food journal is a part of many, many commercial fat-loss programs. Are you suggesting they are kidding their clients?

And you don't have to track every crumb going into your mouth for the rest of your life. It's a tool to make you aware of your eating habits.

I've been keeping my diet log for about 85 days. I quit it two weeks after achieving my dream weight. But my mindfulness is at a high level to this day. I can recall everything I've eaten in the last 24 hours.

So, keep it as long as you need to develop your mindfulness.

## Eat Less Points to Remember

- eating is 80% of success in weight loss
- calorie intake is a grand strategy
- you over-eat
- eating less will fit you, won't kill you - adjust your mindset accordingly
- keep a diet log
- treat a diet log as an indicator of your commitment to lose weight

# Move More

According to the 80/20 rule, to move more is the less critical factor in weight-loss, responsible for only 20% of your results. That's good news for anyone who hates to exercise. It's quite possible and achievable to lose weight without any additional physical activities.

However, as you have to eat, you also have to move. It's impossible to live without those functions. Why don't you use it to your advantage? Each additional pound of muscle will burn an extra 45-50 calories a day. So I encourage you to go and gain those few additional pounds of muscle. The beauty of it is that you need no additional equipment or time to do it. All you need is a mindset which constantly looks for opportunities to move more in your everyday activities, a consciousness about your lifestyle.

Are you going to play with your children? Go and play basketball, instead of a board game.

Are you going to the mall? Park at the farthest parking spot, instead of close to the door.

Are you going to the 3rd floor? Take the stairs, instead

of an elevator.

With an "active mindset" you will find plenty of opportunities to move more. Remember the weight-loss formula:

calories eaten - calories burned = weight loss

Every single additional physical activity brings more burned calories to this equation.

I encourage you to start to work out daily. Bodybuilders insist on exercising every few days, so the muscles can rest and recover. But we are talking here about a few minutes workout, not a bodybuilding. Daily exercise will develop into a habit in half the time, compared to doing it every other day. You can go softly and gently like my wife, who hates moving. Do some aerobic routines for a few minutes every day. Or, you can go hardcore like me - choose an exercise and do a consecutive series to max out.

## HIIT

As I mentioned before, I'm a fan of short and intensive trainings. I figured it out wholly on my own - I was so proud of myself - only to find out that I'm not a fitness genius. There are others who cleared the path long before me. It just shows how detached from anything resembling a healthy lifestyle I was. So, what the heck is HIIT (High-intensity interval training)? According to the definition, it's "an enhanced form of interval training, an exercise strategy alternating periods of short intense anaerobic exercise with less-intense recovery periods," But try to ask how to do it, and you will get almost as many answers as there are people. I've literally seen people arguing on fitness forums:

"That's how you are supposed to do it."

"No man! It's done this way!"

"Guys, what are you talking about? It's not HIIT! Here is the link, where my guru is showing how to do it properly!"

Well, you get the picture. My mentor, Craig Ballantyne, has in his offer a Home Workout Revolution program including a four-minute workout called by a fancy name: "Max Rep Miracle Bodyweight." And, as far as I know, it is the only four-minute workout in his program. Four minutes? For me, it's almost too long.

Try to put a 115-lb. boy on your back, and do pushups for four minutes. Good luck. Or grab a bar and do chin ups for four minutes. Possible, some guys can do just that, but they are not ordinary mortals burdened by 9 to 5 jobs.

The bottom line of HIIT is: it's short, it's intensive. It makes your heart pound; it makes you gasp for air.

So, my very own and original ® way to do a workout is: one consecutive set of bodyweight exercise to your limit. And beyond. It's a little similar to Tabata workout, especially in the case of pushups. I do as much as I can, then I catch my breath on straight arms, and do some more. Straight arms, catch my breath and some more pushups. I do it until I'm breathless and powerless and I can't straighten my arms, I can't heft my body from the floor. It's doable with dips, too, but not in the case of pull ups. That's why I love them – this is the only exercise where my muscles give up before my lungs do.

I'm no fitness trainer, but the results I'm getting aren't too bad. Exercising only by this method, I've beaten Craig Ballantyne in pull-ups. He set a challenge in the Transformation Contest to do the maximum number of pull-ups within 8 minutes. I've beaten him by 6 pull-ups. I prepared myself better for this exercise, and a few days later, I beat him by 19 pull-ups.

I was blown away! He is a professional fitness instructor

— it's his business; it's his life. Me? I have a bar in my apartment and at that time I practiced pull-ups 4-5 times a week, one series of consecutive pull-ups. That's all.

I'm a living example that a very short and intensive workout is at least as effective as long and low-intensive are. So why waste my (and your) valuable time on them?

Since I'm thin and fit, I feel better about myself, so I've actually expanded my workouts. I do my morning HIIT workout as usual, then 2-4 more workouts during the day, and a consecutive series of pull-ups. The reason for this additional exercise is my sweet tooth; thanks to all of those workouts, I am able to burn down a chocolate bar or two.

I recommend a HIIT workout to you. If you value your time, don't spend it on jogging or walking. Well, of course, do spend it on those activities if you enjoy them and you have time for them. But if you look for biggest gains in the least possible time, HIIT is definitely something you should consider.

I do my HIIT workout early in the morning. It has several advantages:

- it is relatively easy to find several minutes for an exercise; you just wake up a few minutes earlier

- you work out on an empty stomach; with high intensity training, it's a blessing. I can never max out, if I have eaten before

- it's easier to structure your morning and develop a habit than to do it later in a day, when your family, friends and job are fighting for your time

- it boosts your metabolism for the few first hours of a day

## Move More Points to Remember

- an additional pound of muscle will burn 45-50 calories a day
- use your everyday activities as opportunities to move more
- exercise daily
- exercise in the morning
- for the fastest results, go for HIIT, if you dare

# Practical Tips

**1.** If you never-ever tried to lose weight, try to start purely from your consciousness and mindset. Ask yourself the questions below every evening before going to bed. It will count as your 'only 10 minutes' given to a weight loss program:

- do I exercise every day? every 2 days? a few times a week? once a week? less than that?
- do I know how many calories I've eaten today?
- did I eat fast food today? any sweets? (if possible, numerate them all)
- did I eat vegetables/fruits today? how many? (if possible, numerate them all)
- how much water do I drink every day? how much today?
- how many hours did I sleep today? what is my average?
- what do I say to myself about my diet? my exercise routine?

If you answered for any self-check question: "I don't know," that's a very honest answer. And it immediately leads to another question, which can create your short-term action plan: How can I become aware of it?

Do this for 30 days in a row and check how this internal, mental activity affects your real world.

**2**. Weigh yourself regularly and in similar circumstances. I weigh myself every Saturday morning, before breakfast and after my morning workout. My cheap, piece-of-supermarket-art scale shows different weights in different locations. It shows 3 different measures, even in the same room. So I do my weighing in a bathroom, where there are stable floor tiles. I weigh myself 3 times and take the average. All this fuss is necessary to get objective information.

If you use different scales, at different places and times of the day, the feedback information you get is almost useless. The same place, the same time, the same circumstances guarantee obtaining quality information.

**3**. Use an online service to educate yourself about foods' nourishment and calories. Almost every weight-loss platform offers a foods library with pictures and such data. Sparkpeople.com, Livestrong.com - to name just a couple.

I recommend http://fatsecret.com - the photos may not be 100% what the text describes at the moment, which can be misleading, but the access is totally free - no registration required.

**4**. Get literate in weight loss & fitness terminology: calories, BMI, carbs, HIIT, Tabata, cardio.

**5**. Move more on a daily basis. Do small, simple things daily: take stairs instead of an elevator; walk to the shop instead of driving; park your car further; put something heavy (like a big bottle of water) into your bag - you will carry additional weight with you - and so on.

Done one time, it doesn't make much of a difference. Done every day, it really compounds over time.

**6**. Ask for advice. I made my own program, learning from my own mistakes. It's a stupid way to learn. A learning curve is much steeper if you learn from the failures and successes of others, too.

At the end of the book, I present a few links to the forums I recommend for this purpose. You'll receive the best advice by being specific about your needs and circumstances. Crappy, generic questions ("How to lose weight?") leads to crappy, generic answers ("Quickly!").

**7**. Find a mentor or an accountability partner online. There are a lot of free weight- loss/fitness forums where people just like you and me share support and experiences.

I recommend the same communities which I pointed out as good sources for seeking advice. People there not only know what they are talking about, they are active and caring, too.

# My Story

Warning! This chapter is highly redundant with the rest of this book. Many (but not all) pieces of my story were included in some chapters above.

My first real action toward losing weight was a daily portion of pushups. I can't pinpoint the exact time when I started doing this exercise, because I've been doing it (with many breaks) for half my life.

I started doing them for the first time in high school, with this thought: "I'll check how many I can do, and I'll do a little more every week." I started with 40.

I dropped it when I was doing about 120 consecutive pushups.

I started again.

I didn't do them for almost the entire time I was studying at the University.

I started again during my first year of full-time work.

Again, I dropped it.

And about 5.5 years ago, I started it once again and I continue to the present day.

I got up to 130 pushups and changed the strategy, because it was very time-consuming. To start with, I put my feet higher (usually on a bed); later I invited my kids to sit on my back.

And guess what? I didn't lose a single pound.

When I was 16 years old, I injured my spine jumping into a swimming pool. It was nothing serious, but when I got fatter, my spine began to hurt. The pain was annoying, coming back again and again in the least expected moments. One time, the pain almost paralyzed me, so I went to a doctor. She gave me powerful pain killers and said I should work on my belly muscles. I liked the idea of sexy abs instead of a bulging gut, so about 2-2.5 years ago, I started to exercise, working on my belly muscles, 5 minutes a day and ended up exercising 15 minutes a day.

Two things happened then. First - I discovered I actually do have time to work out. To tell the truth, I created my time for workouts. I set an alarm clock 15 minutes earlier. I had already been waking up really early - about 5 am - and 15 minutes didn't make much difference.

Second - I started to gain weight. Very slowly, but steadily. My dark secret is that I have a sweet tooth. I could easily eat two pounds of cake in one afternoon.

There are lessons here, but right now, I'm telling my story, not preaching ;)

I started to pay some attention to what I eat. Five years ago, I used to eat four double sandwiches of white bread at work. I also ate breakfast and a late lunch at home. And a doughnut about every 2-3 days. And cakes every time there was an occasion to eat one. And some sweets in the evenings. I cut down on white bread, then I replaced it with a dark bread. That was as far as my diet went. ;)

At the beginning of April 2012, I was 163 lbs. It was my peak point. I was even fatter than on my fat photo - I never used to take half-naked pictures of myself, so the last one I have is from a vacation in 2011. As my spine was in no better shape than a year ago, and pain killers prescribed by a doctor were running out, I made the decision to lose weight.

I faced reality. My exercises alone didn't bring me the desired results. And I had no time to exercise more. I needed to change my strategy. I focused on the second element of a weight loss program - the diet. The first thing I did was cut back my consumption of carbs. I gave up 25% of the bread I used to eat. I introduced more vegetables into my eating schedule. I tried to replace sweets with veggies. What a fight it was! Giving up sweets was a constant struggle, not a one-time battle. And it still is. Thanks to those dietary choices, I got some results. In August 2012, I weighed 154 lbs. Nine pounds in 4.5 months - not the most impressive story you've heard about losing weight, is it?

At the end of August, I read a book, which made me take massive action in order to change my life. I set some goals for the first time since ... I don't know exactly, maybe 1999 when I decided on my university studies? One of those goals was my specific weight at the end of the year. I wanted to be 144 lbs.

I didn't introduce many changes this time. I was just more restrictive in my diet. I cut back sweets almost entirely. I started to eat raw carrots as a snack. I tried to compound small activities to add into calories burning - take a walk instead of driving a car, take stairs instead of an elevator, and so on. At the beginning of December 2012, I reached 145 lbs. and hit a plateau. I hadn't achieve my goal, but I was close.

In January 2013, I introduced one new element into my weight-loss program. I started a diet log. It was not rocket science - I simply wrote down everything I ate and drank which contained any calories. I didn't change my diet. I didn't change my work-out regime. I just kept my mind focused on a task by writing down all I ate.

With that, the plateau had been overcome.

On the 12th of January, I reached 144 lbs. By the 9th of March 2013, I was 138 lbs. I lost what I wanted to lose - 15% of my body weight. Since that date, my goal has been to maintain my weight between 138 and 144 lbs. I can proudly state that I haven't even exceeded 141 lbs. since then.

## In Conclusion

I've already said what I had to say. Now, it's up to you to take my advice and use it in the way best suited to your temperament, schedule and lifestyle. Your neighbor next door did it. You can do it, too. Go for it! I wish you many pounds lost.

# Recommended Resources
## for Weight Loss

I'm an outsider. I stumbled and grappled alone to understand what works and what doesn't. I was curious what people gathered in weight loss/fitness forums have to say about my transition – what would be their advice?

I did some research while writing this book. I posted a quite detailed description of where I was two years ago, and asked them what to do in my circumstances.

*I said:*

I'm 163 lbs., being 5'5" height. It's about 8 lbs. over BMI's normal weight boundary.

I'm out of shape, because I have little to no time for exercise. I have a sedentary job. I commute about 4 hours a day. Playing with my 3 kids is the most exercise I get.

I haven't paid attention to my diet in the past - my bulging gut is proof of that. What is good - I don't eat fast food, my wife cooks for the whole family. What's bad - I love sweets.

I don't want to be fit overnight. I want to lose weight (about 20 lbs.), be fit and stay that way.

Please advise me what would you recommend and especially what does it mean for me in the terms of daily time investment.

## Forums

If you are looking for an online consultation, I recommend you do the same - give many details, so you'll get a high quality response.

I did it in 6 different online communities. Once, I was totally ignored. Once, I had been given just generic advice. Unfortunately, most of communities disappeared during the last seven years. If you want to connect with people who have "been there, done that," find below the forums I recommend:

http://www.fitday.com/fitness/forums/exercise/9672-how-exercise-very-limited-time.html - great feedback, great advice. One guy even recommended the very exercise I've been doing - pushups. I highly recommend this forum.

http://www.weightlossresources.co.uk - it's a paid service with a free trial. The feedback I got there was a very high quality. They advised me exactly what I did right - a diet log, HIIT training and some mindset tips. Everything that I needed to lose weight. And they did it within 24 hours of the free trial. If you are comfortable with a £9.95 monthly fee, go for it!

## More Reading

*The Slight Edge* by Jeff Olson
*The Compound Effect* by Darren Hardy
*Successful Weight Loss Among Obese U.S. Adults* - American Journal of Preventive Medicine

# Learn to Read
# with Great Speed

## How to Take Your Reading Skills
## to the Next Level and Beyond
## in only 10 Minutes a Day

# Introduction

When I started my self-development program, I stumbled upon a workbook about speed reading. The author outlined a program there for a massive improvement in the speed of reading within three months, but you were supposed to practice one to two hours per day, every day.

Two hours per day! That's a lot of commitment. I didn't have time for it. But I was at a stage of developing my Ten-Minute Philosophy and decided to give it a try, but only for 10 minutes a day. I took that program and modified it by extending each week into a full twelve weeks.

The last time I checked my reading speed, I read at about 240 words per minute. Since that time, my skills had no chance to improve, as I was reading less rather than more and neglected any training in that area.

I checked my results after a month from starting my 10-minute practices, and I was blown away! It was 360 words per minute, 50% progress! Later on, it appeared this result was a coincidence, but still, after six weeks of practice, I read about 340 words per minute, and the progress was impressive.

All you need to achieve similar results is the information

in this book and 10 minutes a day of your time.

I want to help you, not to rob you. If you can already read quickly, or if you read no more than 30 minutes a day, then the program described below won't improve your skills or give you profits. Remember that I speak of all the time you commit to reading as a whole. That includes Internet, magazines, mail, and work materials, not just reading for pleasure in your leisure time.

So, reader, how fast do you read? If you don't know, then check it out immediately:

http://www.readingsoft.com/
OR
http://www.freereadingtest.com/

If you are offline and cannot reach those online tests, then prepare a timer, and read the four paragraphs highlighted below in a different font. Start a timer, and read the paragraphs at a fast enough pace to comprehend the meaning. Then, use the formula I provided after those paragraphs to gauge your reading speed. Ready? Go:

If your honest result is below two hundred and fifty words per minute, then this book is the best value available for you. Grab it, practice ten minutes a day, and within several weeks, you will experience a significant improvement of your reading skills.

If you read below four hundreds words per minute, then I still encourage you to give my ten-minute program a try. You don't have much to lose, and you have a lot to gain: your precious time. You could read the same amount of text in 2/3 of time previously needed. Or you can read twenty, forty, or one hundred percent more text at the same time.

If you read faster than four hundred words per minute, then I cannot guarantee that the techniques I recommend will significantly improve your reading speed. But if you've never consciously worked on your reading skills, then chances are that you have a natural talent and you can develop it with a few simple, consistent exercises. Try it for thirty days. All you've got to lose is one dollar and five hours of your time within a month. The average American spends more time in front of the TV in two days[1] And the potential gains are huge.

Generally, the slower you read right now, the bigger potential gain you can make. Before I started deliberately improving my reading speed, I could read two hundred and forty words per minute and I read about two hours every day. I increased my reading speed by fifty percent - while only practicing ten minutes a day. Thanks to my improved skill, I can absorb twenty-two and a half hours of additional material monthly during my two hours of daily reading. Or, I can read the same amount in less time, and use the remaining hours in other ways. If I used them for additional work at my current wages, I could earn an additional two hundred and ten dollars monthly.

On your timer, you have the number of seconds it took you to read the above 344 words. Convert the minutes into seconds, if necessary, and count the words per minute.

Use this formula: **344 / number of seconds * 60**

Now you know your reading speed and can make a rational decision about improving it by implementing my advice. Use my Speed Reading Profits Calculator to check your potential gains.

Provide your reading tempo (words per minute) and

---

1. http://www.bls.gov/news.release/atus.nr0.htm; American Time Use Survey Summary 2012, Bureau of Labor Statistics, US Department of Labor

how much time you spend reading every day in minutes. If you also add your hourly wage, you will see a monetary equivalent of the time saved.

Go and see for yourself: http://www.expandbeyondyourself.com/tools/srpcalc

Using my very conservative assumptions, here are some profitability boundaries regarding a 10-minute daily speed reading practice:

| A reading tempo (words per minute) | Estimated improvement achieved by 10-minute practice | Daily time spend on reading (minutes) |
|---|---|---|
| Less than 250 | 50% | 31 |
| From 250 to 300 | 40% | 37 |
| From 300 to 350 | 30% | 45 |
| From 350 to 400 | 20% | 65 |
| More than 400 | 10% | 120 |

If you read less than 30 minutes a day, it is pointless to invest 10 minutes and increase your reading speed by 50%. You'll read faster, but you'll also reduce your reading time because of practice. However, you may make bigger progress than me: 60% or 160% and still get a positive net result. It's your call.

On the other hand, the more you read, the more profitable an increase of your reading skill will be. If I read four hours a day, I would save one working week per month.

## Conclusion

Check out your reading speed. Estimate how much time you spend reading on average. Find out if a 10-minute practice is viable for you.

# Speed Reading Obstacles

Unfortunately, the vast amount of knowledge we have gathered as humans seems to guarantee that we have at least two opinions about every single thing. Just look at the various diets and fitness strategies: eat that - no, eat this; eat in the morning - no, eat in the afternoon; eat fruits on an empty stomach - no, use them as snacks; run or walk steadily for half an hour every day - no, use five minute HIIT training every second day. It seems we can't agree on anything. It's the same with speed reading.

One study shows that sub-vocalization is an unavoidable part of reading process and doesn't affect reading speed; another shows that it's necessary to reduce it to the point of elimination to improve reading speed. One shows that listening to music while reading can improve your speed; another that it slows you down.

Frankly, I don't care what the latest research "proved" this time. I'm a practitioner. So, I'm teaching what worked in my case and in the case of other people with whom I have contact. I have no interest in the opinions of eggheads as long as they are contradictory to each other, and especially when they are contradictory with my experiences.

Thus, I do not quote authorities and research studies in this book. I just show you what my beliefs are, what techniques I use ... and what results I get.

Ok, so now let's go for the reasons of less than optimal reading speed.

## Sub Vocalization

Sub-vocalization, or silent speech, is defined as the internal speech made when reading a word, thus allowing the reader to imagine the sound of the word as it is read. This is a natural process when reading - but **only** because we all were taught to read by vocalization first.

Sub-vocalization is popularly associated with moving one's lips; the actual term refers primarily to the movement of muscles associated with speaking, not the literal moving of lips. Most sub-vocalization is done just inside our heads and is undetectable even by the person doing the sub-vocalizing.

The definition of sub-vocalization that I found states also that it "helps to reduce cognitive load, and it helps the mind to access meanings to enable it to comprehend and remember what is read." And I say, "That's B.S."

I achieved the biggest improvement in reading speed by applying the sub-vocalization reducing exercises. We don't read through our ears; we read through our eyes. "Translating" letters and words to sounds slows us down. When we do that, the talking speed reduces our reading speed. Speed reading is about getting information straight from the sheet of paper (or a screen) through our eyes to our brain. Sense of hearing as a go-between is redundant.

## Fixation

Reading is not a process of recognizing a text word by word; it's recognizing the meaning of the words in context.

| Try to | Isn't it a | easily | your eyes |
|--------|-----------|--------|-----------|
| read this | mental effort | comprehend | run all over |
| text normally | making your | those sentences | the text |
| as usual, | head spin? | in that way. | and your mind |
| from left | It's very | You are | is trying to |
| to right. | difficult to | confused, | figure the meaning out. |

Most of us don't realize that the eye sees the picture **only** when it is motionless. While reading, if the eye "jumps" from one part of text to another, it's called an eye fixation. The more fixations you do, the slower you read. There are a few elements which determine your number of fixations.

## Vision Span

Your eye's efficiency is very important in the reading process. If your vision span is wider, you can read more words per fixation. That means fewer fixations per text line and higher speed of reading. And opposite dependency is also true - since each fixation equals less words read, then the more fixations per line equals slower reading progress. Vision span is a physical attribute, and it can be trained.

## Vocabulary

To see how vocabulary determines eye fixations, try to read the verses below carefully, to get their meaning:

*Sownynge in moral vertu was his speche,*
*And gladly wolde he lerne, and gladly teche.*

Those lines come from "The Cantebury Tales", written in Middle English in the 14th century by Geoffrey Chaucer.

You had problems with comprehending this text because some of the words are not in your vocabulary. When you are not familiar with a text, you read and you don't know the words used, your eyes stop frequently to recognize the unfamiliar meaning and the number of fixations increases.

When you don't need to dwell on specific words, you read more words in one fixation, which allows you to read faster.

Compare your speed of understanding Middle English verses with the speed of reading below:

*Filled with moral virtue was his speech,*
*And gladly would he learn, and gladly teach.*

It was much easier and faster this time, wasn't it?

## Topic Familiarity

Your background, your education, your interests, your general knowledge - all these factors influence your reading speed, because they determine your vocabulary and your reading confidence. When the topic is familiar to you, is in your area of expertise or field of interest, you are at home with the author's terminology. The overall meaning is obvious to you, so again, you don't dwell on individual words, and you need fewer fixations to read a single line. Thus, you read faster.

It explains the paradox of correlation between reading speed and comprehension. The lesser understanding of text leads to the slower reading. On the other hand, the faster you read, the more you can read and you can get familiar with more subjects.

## Regression

It simply means back-tracking, re-reading text that you've already read. It's like taking two steps forward and one step back with your eyes. The reasons for regression can differ from one case to another: lack of concentration, really difficult text to comprehend, an excessive sub-vocalization – which disrupts the process of reading – or just bad reading habits.

## Other

Different "schools" of speed reading numerate many different additional reasons: lack of concentration, lighting, lack of selection and anticipation skills, and lack of reading tactics. All of these are obvious generalizations or some extensions of sub-vocalization, fixation or regression.

For example, a lack of concentration. Well, it's normal that you get worse results if you are not concentrating, no matter if you read or make burgers at McDonald's. Lighting is important – you cannot read in the dark, can you? Selection and anticipation skills are related to topic familiarity and vocabulary. You cannot select main points from a text when you don't know what it is talking about; you cannot anticipate the meaning of words when your vocabulary is poor. Undeveloped selection and anticipation skills also drive you into regression – if you don't fully comprehend what you read, you try to get the meaning by re-reading a fragment of the text.

# Techniques

The way we learn to read is the cause of every problem we have with speed reading. It is like our training had been aborted in the middle. We all learn at school to read by going through various stages: first recognizing the letters, then joining them into groups and spelling them out, then reading out loud to get a smoothness in reading skill, and finally, we learn to read internally, using our mind's voice. And our teachers are perfectly comfortable with that.

"Can Johnny read?"
"Yes."
"Great! Next one!"

And we are left at this socially acceptable level of reading skill.

I say, if some simple techniques were to be introduced into primary school's syllabus, all children would have improved reading speed.

I will numerate a few techniques to fight off every speed reading obstacle and explain which I've chosen them for my practice and why.

## Sub Vocalization

To reduce sub-vocalization, you need to stop using your sense of hearing to read. All of the exercises below help you to replace the old, slow "see–say–hear–think" way of reading with the faster "see–think" habit of **thinking word meanings**.

## Bite Your Tongue

It is a first, basic technique. It is possible to apply only if you read really slowly, and you are able to observe that you are trying to articulate words while reading - you murmur or move your tongue, consciously or subconsciously.

My son, who used to read very slowly, used this technique successfully.

## Occupy Your Internal Voice with Another Task

- count aloud as you read "1, 2, 3, 4, 5, 6" and so on
- hum
- sing something simple like "la-la-la-la"
- recite simple and very deeply memorized text
- beat a rhythm as you read. This is my favorite

I have no intention of acting like a blusterous lunatic while reading. I read mostly at work or in a public transport. There are people around me most of the time. But beating a rhythm is a whole different story. It is unobtrusive, so I read and pat my thigh rhythmically.

What is more, the workbook's author claims this method is the most difficult and most effective for reducing sub-vocalization. Nothing but advantages - so I adopted it.

I just recall some melody and use its rhythm. I found also that actually hearing a rhythm is not necessary. I travel in noisy trains and buses a lot. Sometimes, so noisy that I can't hear my own patting. But the act of patting makes me concentrate on a rhythm and hear the "sound" of the rhythm in my head.

It's important to use your whole forearm, not just a wrist. Beating transfers a part of your attention from the hearing sense to your body motion.

Don't get frustrated if the art of reading and occupying your internal voice simultaneously eludes you. It's normal. You will lose a rhythm focusing too much on comprehending a text. You will beat a rhythm perfectly, but you will lose an ability to focus on reading. You will have no idea what you have just read after the exercise. The same is true with other tactics - recitation, singing, humming, and counting aloud.

## Sub Vocalization Conclusion

Using one of the above techniques is obligatory if you want to improve your reading speed. Sub-vocalization is the number one enemy of speed reading. "See–say–hear–think" is a detour we have been taught as children, and it will not serve you right in adulthood. Breaking this habitual detour is a pesky experience, but the results are well worth it.

## Fixation

There are lots of causes of a greater number of fixations, so there is no single simple remedy to fix it. Whatever the people behind the speed reading industry – the people who are selling the books, programs, and courses say – nobody can substitute for you. You are the one who needs to work on your vocabulary or topic familiarity.

Techniques can help you only in the "technical" aspect. You can expand your vision span with exercises, but it won't do you much good, if you don't understand every third word in some professional periodical.

## Eye-Span Pyramid

There are different kinds of pyramids - with single words, sentences, and numbers. You are supposed to read them from the apex to the bottom, keeping your view in the middle of the pyramid.

The vertical moves of eyeballs are not allowed.

This

exercise

will help you

to expand your vision

span by working on your

peripheral vision. You can read

more words at a time when your vision span is wider

When the text is too wide for you to read it with one fixation, then stop, close your eyes for a few seconds, open them again focusing your view in the middle of the pyramid, and try to see as many words as possible on the both sides of the line.

## Shultz Tables

This is a tool to train your vision span. A table consists of 25 fields filled with symbols. They are usually numbers, but they also can be letters or any kind of symbols that can be arranged in a specific order. Doing exercises with Shultz tables develops your three-dimensional, multi-channeled attention. The symbols in the table will subconsciously be perceived as one picture.

Your purpose is to concentrate your view on the center field, whilst being able to see the central number and all the numbers in the corners of a table. Locate the numbers in ascending or descending order as fast as you can, keeping your view focused on the central square of the table.

| 6 | 13 | 19 | 17 | 2 |
|---|---|---|---|---|
| 11 | 22 | 8 | 25 | 23 |
| 18 | 16 | 1 | 20 | 12 |
| 14 | 10 | 24 | 15 | 5 |
| 4 | 7 | 21 | 9 | 3 |

At the beginning, you can start with smaller tables - 3x3 or 4x4 fields. You should be able to point out all numbers in less than one minute.

Try to find the numbers faster with each successive exercise.

I like Shultz tables the most of all the exercises expanding the field of vision. They are relatively easy to create, and numbers in each of them are arranged in a random manner. It is not so easy to randomly create pyramids or columns of words or numbers.

I found some PDF documents, printed them and used them for the practice sessions. After several iterations, I had all the text and numbers memorized and couldn't use them effectively.

## Fixation Training

The next stage of expanding your vision span is to create a fixation habit. To have a wide vision span is fine and good, but we were taught to read a text word by word, so we need to develop new reading habits - to jump just a few times over a text line with our eyesight. I've just started this kind of training - this is as far as my personal program has gotten so far.

You should develop the habit of moving your eyesight just a couple times per line. I used pre-prepared texts and, more or less, I memorized them. To work on a new text with every practice session, you need a template with dots marking the stopping points for your eye. It's a little fuss to copy a new text to a template file and print it every time, but it's much better than working on a text you've already read several times.

This kind of reading also helps tremendously with fighting off a regression. You consciously force yourself to read chunks of text jumping from one to another, and there is no going back in this method. You train this way of reading as long as it's necessary to develop a new subconscious habit.

## Fixation: Conclusion

No "technical" exercises will help you to enrich your vocabulary or general knowledge. You must work on them on your own. If you worked on some text previously a couple of times, the training of your eyes transforms into the training of your memory. You need a source of fresh reading materials for your practice sessions.

## Regression

Regression can slow you down significantly. If you read very fast, but you need to go back and re-read the text you've just gone through, then in consequence, you read at a mediocre pace.

The picture below illustrates how your eyes are working when a regression takes place:

What you need instead, is steady movement in one direction. Always forward.

## Selection

Conscious control over your attention is an important part of speed reading. Selection, paying attention to a specific purpose, is a skill that can help you to decide if scanned text is useful for you and worth reading or not. This is especially important in the Internet era.

Selection exercises are really simple, and I love them because you can work on any text. Well, almost any – the text you practice on must be new to you.

## Exercises:

- within five seconds, find a repeated word in a text. Read the text to the end, counting the occurrences of this word
- find all the articles in a text
- find all the numbers in a text
- find all the connectives in a text
- find all the verbs in a text

You can establish your own criteria of selection. The only limit is your creativity. It all comes down to finding something in a text. You can also add a time factor to the exercises; for example, you have only 20 seconds to find all the articles on a page.

## Pointer

I left the best for last. Using a pointer to read has a multitude of advantages. It helps to eliminate regression, reduce sub-vocalization, and to master your eye fixation. It is THE technique of speed reading.

Using a pointer is the most powerful and easiest way to eliminate a regression. Use the tip of your finger or a pen. Point it below the line of text and move it as you read in a sweeping motion, just like kids who learn to read. Oh, a little faster than them. You don't have to point the whole length of a line, your peripheral vision will take care of the beginnings and ends of the lines.

Reading above the speed of your usual comprehension rate with a pointer reduces sub-vocalization. Your internal voice just cannot cope with your pointer.

Pursuing the pointer with your eyesight, especially faster than you are used to reading, trains your eyes to catch chunks of sentences, not individual words.

This one simple tool may have an enormous influence on your reading skill progress.

If you read mostly on a computer screen - like me - don't worry. Use the pointer for your practice sessions and whenever you lay hands on a paper copy. The progress might not be as rapid as you wish, but there will be some progress, nonetheless. Your exercises with physical books will improve your screen reading, too.

You can also use a pointer to read from eReader devices, unless they have touch panels. But there is a work-around for such devices, too – just hover the pointer a quarter of an inch over the device. By the way, that's the way I prefer to use a pointer. I find the swish of the finger on a paper sheet a bit distracting.

My workbook encouraged me to start by sweeping the pointer every second line, and try to read two lines at a time, then to read three, four, and more, and then go to even more advanced techniques.

## Regression: Conclusion

There are other, more advanced techniques for eliminating regression, but I haven't used them yet. And I'm already 10 months into my 10-minute speed reading program. They are not needed at the beginning; there is a lot of time for you to look for them later.

You can train selection on any unknown text.

Using the pointer is the simplest and most powerful speed reading technique (if you can even call it technique). It's just something we don't usually do during "ordinary" reading, but we should.

Don't worry if you read mostly from a computer screen; use the pointer for your practice sessions only, and it will impact your screen reading, too.

## Super-Speed Exercises

Those exercises are not humanly possible to execute, especially the first one, when your task is to read a little faster than your record. Even if you read 4,700 words per minute (about world record), you should exercise reading faster than that.

The goal of those exercises is to strain your "reading muscle" so it can grow.

**1.** The whole single iteration of this exercise takes about 8-10 minutes.

a) for one minute, read with a speed greater than 100 words per minute than your actual record

b) for one minute, read with a speed greater than 100 words per minute than in point a)

c) for one minute, read with a speed greater than 100 words per minute than in point b)

d) for one minute, read with a speed greater than 100

words per minute than in point c)

e) for one minute, read with a speed greater than 100 words per minute than in point d)

f) for one minute, read with comprehension as fast as you can

**2.** This exercise takes about 20 minutes. I only do it on weekends, when I can organize more time for my practice sessions.

a) for one minute, read using a pointer with a speed of 2,000 words per minute. Sweep the pointer every three, four, or more lines. Mark the point where you finished reading. I used "Iliad" and "Odyssey" for this practice. I figured out that one page contains about 250 words, so I was supposed to read eight pages within a minute.

b) read again the same fragment of text as in point a), but use 4 minutes this time

c) read again the same fragment of text within 3 minutes

d) read again the same fragment of text within 2 minutes

e) read for 5 minutes in a way described in point a) from the text you marked onward (it was 40 more pages in my case)

f) for one minute read with comprehension as fast as you can

**3.** This exercise takes about 5-6 minutes.

a) start from beginning of the chapter: scan the text using the pointer; you have 4 seconds to scan each page

b) read the text scanned in point a) with the speed of 2000 words per minute

c) for one minute, read with comprehension as fast as you can

**4.** The whole single iteration of this exercise takes less than 3 minutes.

a) for one minute, read as fast as you can; don't care about comprehending what you read

b) for one minute, read with comprehension as fast as you can

# Program

The first thing to do is to gauge your reading speed. You probably already know this after reading Chapter One.

The results you get can vary from one test to another. They are dependent not only on your level of reading skill, but also on external conditions: lighting, noise level and so on. Even your mood and the kind of text on which you are taking a test can influence the results.

My reading speed varies from 360 to 510 words per minute – the difference is huge, isn't it?

I recommend that you gauge your reading speed at least once a week, ideally in the same circumstances. For example, in the morning next to the window, with a lot of sunlight. Or, you can measure it every day and take the average. I don't recommend this approach, because gauging takes time, too, and we are talking about a 10-minute program here.

If you are determined to measure your reading speed every day, I recommend using the below, approximated (and fast) method:

- count the number of words on five consecutive full lines of print. (for example, 55 words on five lines)
- divide this by 5 to get an average number of words per line. (for example, 11 words per line)
- set the timer for a minute
- read for one minute and count the number of lines (for example, 35 lines read)
- multiple the number of lines you have read by the average words per line (for example, 35*11=385 words per minute)

For more gauging methods, visit my blog.

Use easy and interesting lectures for your practices. I practice on books "I've always wanted to read, but have never had time."

"Warm up" your eyes. It is supposed to sharpen your vision and activate your peripheral sight. Just trace the geometric figure or infinity symbol with your eyes alone and then switch, moving your eyes in the other direction. Experts advise to do it for one minute; I do it for 10 to 20 seconds before each practice session.

I remind you that I've tailored an intensive speed reading self-course to 10 minute practices. You can do the same with my program.

For example, you can use 30 minutes for daily practices and shrink every program's stage to one month.

## Stage 1. Months one to three

1. Reducing the sub-vocalization.
Check out the techniques I described in chapter 4. Try various methods, and choose the one best suited for you.

2. Super speed exercise number 1.
I recommend to practice it 1-2 times a week. Remember, use the pointer.

## Stage 2. Months four to six

1. Continue exercises for reducing the sub-vocalization.
   - if you have chosen some other method, try the rhythm beating exercise once a week; it is supposed to be the most effective way to fight off sub-vocalization.
   - focus on the comprehension
2. Selection exercises.
3. Super speed exercise number 2.

## Stage 3. Months seven to nine

1. Eye span training.
- Shultz tables
- eye span pyramids
2. Super speed exercise number 3.

## Stage 4. Months ten to twelve.

1. Continue the eye span widening exercises.
2. Fixation training.
3. Super speed exercise number 4.

## A Call to Action

That's as far as my training goes. Nothing fancy, is it? You may find other good, solid advice on how to arrange your speed reading practice sessions:

- secure the proper environment: lighting, peace and quiet for your sessions
- concentrate
- sit upright
- be alone
- use the professional tools and programs
- take care of your mental attitude: realize the goal of every session and overall program, set your mind to do the exercises to the best of your abilities
- set your own goals and deadlines

All of this is fine, all is good, but there is one missing ingredient: you. All that advice can discourage you. It looks like a lot of fuss, doesn't it? You must prepare: close yourself in your private office, meditate to clear and focus your mind, and then, practice speed reading, for 19 minutes. Do you feel motivated by such a picture?

The above advice is important but not critical. You can practice in a noisy environment; you can practice with inappropriate lighting; you can practice with diminished focus; or you can be discouraged. How do I know? Well, I've been there, done that.

I'm occupied with so many projects that I have no time to arrange my speed reading practice sessions. I practice on the fly - while commuting, whenever I read something which demands less than 100% of my attention (I developed a beating habit). I can practice in a "sterile atmosphere" only on weekends, when I wake up before other family members, and I do my super speed exercises in peace and quiet.

You will fail **only** if you don't practice. The whole idea of this book is to show you that speed reading is not rocket science. In fact, it's quite mundane. And it's easy. Do you know Jim Rohn's definition of "easy?" It's something you can do.

And in fact, you can do it. It's just like your reading education had been aborted halfway in primary school. My 10-year-old son improved his reading speed by more than double what it had been – are your skills worse than a child's? Ten minutes a day is enough to observe some progress within a few weeks. It's worth it. You can read more. You can spend less time on reading. You can use the saved time to play with your children, spend it with your spouse, or do whatever else you want.

So start. Persevere. Keep practicing. It will feel awkward, especially at the beginning. You won't grasp what you read on your early sessions, or on super speed exercises. Don't worry. Keep pushing. Remember, daily sustained action brings results. It's a law of nature.

# Free Resources

There are a lot of books, courses, and computer programs on the Internet regarding speed reading. Some of them advertise their services giving some free resources. And you English speakers are blessed with useful tools freely available on the Net.

While writing this book, I've done some research and found several amazing tools for English readers. I will also give you some links to my own resources. I can't guarantee that the tools that are not mine will be available and free forever - those are just some resources I stumbled upon during my research.

Those are not affiliate links, I am not trying to sell you anything. I didn't test any paid services on these sites. I just tested some free tools and found them helpful. Below, I'll list them and comment on how you can use them.

## http://spreeder.com/app.php?intro=1

A very useful tool for fixation training. I love its flexibility - you can set the reading speed, the number of fixations, number of words per fixation and a few more things. The best feature is that you can train each time on a different text. You just press the "New" button and paste your text. The only critical remark I have is that the window with the text is not very wide, and the text can be broken in a weird way.

You can also use it for super speed exercises 1 and 2.

## https://etc.usf.edu/techease/4all/learning/using-the-readability-extension-for-firefox-and-chrome/

The ReadAbility extension is a great tool to improve your comfort with online reading. It converts any web page into a plain, black and white nicely formatted presentation of the text. It removes all distractions - ads, links, unnecessary images, and videos.

It doesn't work perfectly - on one portal it generated the same article three times for me. You can use it as an add-on to the Firefox or Chrome browser.

## http://fasterreader.eu/pages/en/index-en.html

There are a whole bunch of tools there, most of them Java-based, which can cause trouble in the Firefox browser.

- a fine tool for selection training

- a tool for warming up your eyes - use it before practice if you practice in front of a computer.

- a fine tool for vision span training on Shultz's tables, with the element of a game. Unfortunately, clicking on numbers upsets your concentration on the center of the table.

## http://www.expandbeyondyourself.com/img/warmup.jpg

- figures for warm up exercises on my site; you can print it and use for offline practices; just follow the dots with your eyesight very fast in one direction, then again in another direction.

## http://expandbeyondyourself.com/tools/szultz

- Shultz's tables generator hosted on my site; it generates random tables for offline practice.

I use them for my own practices. It's not very user friendly, but it does its job. I prefer the 5x5 dimensions of the tables.

To generate a new set of tables, just press the "back" button in the browser and press the "generate" button once again. Try different browsers and different printer settings to get an ideal size on the paper sheet.

# The Stories

I've promised you stories, so here they are. Most of mine you know from the first chapter, although I've filled in some blanks. I include my son's story, also. Nathaniel is 10 years old and had significant problems with reading. He more than doubled his reading speed within eight months.

## Nathaniel's Story

At the first parent teacher meeting of the school year of 2012-2013, (18th of October 2012) I discovered that my son was neglecting his school work. Let's keep quiet about the home scene which took place after the meeting. It was too ugly to be printed ;)

Anyway, I decided to pay more attention to his learning. He hated to read. In fact, he hated it so much that we used to give him reading assignments as a punishment.

The day after the parent-teacher meeting, I gauged his reading speed. The result were very poor, even for ten years old - just 71 words per minute. He had been sub-vocalizing quite audibly, murmuring under his nose. So, we started a reading practice program. He first had to read five, then ten pages a day. I advised him to bite his tongue while reading.

We did a next test of his reading speed on the last day of October. He improved to 100 words per minute within twelve days. A 42% increase; not too bad.

At the end of November, he read 130 words per minute. I set him the goal for the end of January: 150 words per minute. But he got stuck. He was still below this boundary at the end of March.

I insisted on a technique he doesn't like - beating rhythmically while reading, as I got great results doing it rigorously. He has been doing it very unwillingly.

In the middle of April, we were preparing for another speed reading test, when I proposed this: "Use your finger as a pointer." This is another basic technique, but I had never mentioned it before. I had been focusing on eliminating his excessive sub-vocalization, neglecting other enemies of speed reading.

"OK" - he agreed hesitantly.

BAM! His result was 170 words per minute!

It was a great result.

So, we made an agreement. From then on, I would not supervise his reading. He could read as much (or not as much) as he wanted. I scheduled the next test at the end of May, and he happily neglected his speed reading training. He trained maybe 10 times within the whole month. Every sustained action brings results, but his action was not consistent. His reading speed dived below 170 words per minute again.

The next test, on the 10th of May, didn't show any improvement, so I again made him read every day. At the end of May, he read 192 words per minute – his best results so far.

He read all seven parts of *The Chronicles of Narnia* and

four other books during the training process - more books than 70% of Americans, ages 16 and up, read in 2012[1].

## My story

When I started my self-development program, I'd stumbled upon a workbook about speed reading. The author outlined a program there for a massive improvement in the speed of reading within three months, but you were supposed to practice 1-2 hours per day, every day.

Two hours per day! That's a lot of commitment. About 25% of my available time. And I need that time to commute, to spend with family, to pray, and to learn other skills. Out of the question.

But I had fresh in my mind all the examples of consistent fruitful efforts from my past, so I gave my 10 minutes philosophy a chance.

"I'll only practice fast reading for 10 minutes a day," I decided. Why not? It was just 10 minutes. I modified the program, extending each week into 12 weeks.

The program, from the workbook I found, starts with exercises eliminating sub-vocalization. I read a lot, so I have plenty of opportunities to practice, but beating rhythmically while reading made me dizzy. Either I didn't understand what I was reading, or I couldn't keep the rhythm. One way or another, the practice was no fun. Nevertheless, I stuck with this exercise for a few weeks.

The last time I had checked my reading speed was during my university study. I read about 240 words per minute. Since that time, my skills had no chance to improve, as I was reading less rather than more and neglected any

1. http://libraries.pewinternet.org/2012/12/27/e-book-reading-jumps-print-book-reading-declines/

training in that area.

I checked my results after a month from starting my 10-minute practice, and I was blown away! It was 360 words per minute, a 50% progress! One month, 30 short sessions of practice, and I was able to read 50% more books in the same time. Later on, it appeared this result was just coincidence. Reading speed varies from one test to another; it is dependent on the text I'm testing on, my mood, and external circumstances. But still, after six weeks of practice, I read about 340 words per minute, and the progress was impressive.

You can't even imagine what it meant to me. I'm a reader. I had read thousands of books with my meager 240-words-per-minute speed. Suddenly, I felt like a kid in a candy store when a 50% bargain sale was announced. To get the picture of my state at that moment, try to recall Gollum from the Lord of the Rings, drooling and lisping, "my presssscious."

From that moment on, I had no hesitation at all. I've been going through the next stages of the program, without flinching. I used the practice sessions to read some classic books I had never had time for: Homer's Iliad and Odyssey, Clausewitz's On War, Napoleon Hill's Think and Grow Rich, and several others. I am reading Marcus Aurelius' Meditations now.

When it came to the selection skill practices, I used those sessions to read *Early to Rise* newsletters, which had piled up in my mailbox. I skipped the text looking for the articles or conjunctions, and I was able to get the meaning, by the way.

My results have regularly been above 360 words per minute for several months. My best result was was 511 words per minute, and I often reach over 400.

# Conclusion

When I read the stories of people who improved their reading skills by 100% within a few weeks, I feel a little dumb. My progress is meager and slow compared to them. But I really practice just 10 minutes a day. I do 90% of my reading on a computer screen; the only pointer I can use, in this case, is a mouse cursor, and it is not the most comfortable tool for this job.

I'm living proof that a 10-minute practice can be fruitful. I can read more than 50% of what I read a year ago within the same time. I can read 90 minutes a day (including the speed reading practices) and still read the same amount of text that used to take me two hours to read a year ago.

You can do it, too.

Do yourself a favor. Save your reading time for more interesting activities. Read much more in the same amount of time, and improve your skills and knowledge. And you can get much better and more rapid results than me.

Practice 20 minutes a day, instead of 10. Practice in optimal conditions, not on noisy, crowded buses. Just be more serious in your training than I was, and you are bound to progress faster.

Value your time.

Your time is your life. Start today, grab a book and use your finger as a pointer, or read and simultaneously pat your thigh rhythmically. Just for ten minutes. Discover that there is no magic in speed reading and keep practicing.

# Contact Me

I'd love to know your reading skills progress and see that my work has helped you some way, so please send me a simple email saying, "I used to read xxx words per minute, and now I read yyy wpm,"... to:

**michal@expandbeyondyourself.com.**

That's all I need, although any other feedback is always welcomed as well. You can also follow me at:

**www.expandbeyondyourself.com**

# RELEASE
## YOUR KID'S DORMANT
# GENIUS
## IN JUST TEN MINUTES A DAY

PARENTING
YOUR SMART UNDERACHIEVER
WITH CONSISTENCY AND LOVE

# Disclaimer

I'm not an American. In an attempt to make the book more readable for you, I've "Americanized" the most 'native' parts of this book. I've changed some subjects' names. In Poland, we have a different scale of school grades; I translated it into what's most common in the USA.

My elder son's name is Krzysztof and it's pronounced as "Cshishtoff," but in English, it's Christopher. My younger son's name is written in Polish differently than in English - Nataniel.

This is the 3rd book in the series - which were originally published separately. You'll find that some material in the second chapter is also in *The Fitness Expert Next Door* and *Learn to Read with Great Speed.*

# Introduction

When you are trying to help out with your kid's learning for the first time, you need to recognize and work on his/her weak spots. At least, my experience confirms that this approach bears good fruits. I focused on improving Nathaniel's weak spots. This method not only enhanced those particular skills and areas he had troubles with, but it also brought overall improvement of his school situation.

Did you ever fail and were disappointed by your results? Did you ever put yourself in a self-criticism spiral? Well, kids have the same inner critic's mechanism, and it works in the case of their school results, too:

"I suck at English. I'll never learn it. I'm a failure. I don't want to learn it anymore; it's pointless."

So when we improved the areas he didn't feel confident in, his horizon expanded. I observed his childish joy when he understood English enough to construct simple sentences, or when he doubled his reading speed.

His inner talk changed, too. He discovered he can learn, he can improve, he can achieve more, even in areas where he didn't think he could. Because of this new attitude, he corrected grades in not only a few subjects, but virtually all the subjects.

Do not try to improve your child's strong points to instill more confidence in him/her or whatever the reason you've come up with. I think it's fine and good, a noble intent, but only if you have time and resources for such activities. As I said in the previous chapter, I assume you have enough on your plate and it's hard for you to find more time to take care of your kid's teaching. And I assure you, your child will cope with his strong points, without breaking a sweat.

My son is very good in math. He was 26th in the countrywide competition (I don't know the exact number, but there were several tens of thousands of competitors). Regarding math, he knows his value and has been getting "As" for most of his life. His small successes fueled his confidence. His motivation was (and still is) high. He didn't need my help in that area.

However, I could train him to be even better. I saw that with some consistency, he could achieve more, but then I wouldn't have any time for training his other skills, the ones which desperately cried for improvement.

I don't know about you, how much you know about your kid's struggles, but I didn't really know what the exact problems were regarding my son's education. I had some vague concepts and they weren't even far from the reality - for example, I knew he despised reading, but I had no idea how poorly he read. What I mean is that I was familiar with his problem areas - calligraphy, reading, spelling, fluent speech, English (a foreign language for him). I just didn't realize the full scope of his problems.

And the same may be true in your case. You know what's wrong - sometimes it's enough to take a look at a child's grades to know that - but you don't know the details.

So get to know them.

You don't need fancy tests or professional counseling. Not that they don't work or would be harmful - it's just an additional fuss, time and resources to sacrifice, and you can use this time to start immediately. I needed more than a month to reserve an appointment at the Learning Disabilities Service. It would be wasted time if I just sat on my hands that whole period.

I started doing Nathaniel's homework with him regularly. I think it's the easiest and most efficient way to get familiar with your child's level of skills and knowledge. He/she must do it anyway, so why not use this as an excuse to get some useful intel? And my experience is that the kid's problems are not enormous. Every adult would recognize and deal with them with ease. Let's take a look at what I found out about my son's weak spots:

- Reading - I had just started my speed reading training then, so I checked Nathaniel's reading speed out of curiosity. He read only 71 words per minute! I found the source of all his troubles with reading by this single masterstroke. The slower you read, the less you comprehend (at least it's true up to about 200 words per minute). He read so slowly that he couldn't follow the references for math exercises. He generally didn't read any exercise's description; he had been guessing or asking schoolmates and teachers for the meaning.

- English - I knew he was not very good at it, but he had been getting "B" most of the times, sometimes "Cs" and occasionally even an "A". Frankly, I don't know how he got them. Was it his cleverness? Or the fact that he had about five different English teachers during the first three years? I discovered that he knew just a handful of words, maybe five dozen. He had no idea how to construct a negative sentence – he didn't even know how to alter "to be."

- Spelling - Polish is a difficult language with native characters and complicated writing rules. Nathaniel had problems with them, too, but he had even been writing people's and place's names with small letters. It's not that he didn't know the rules, he just completely ignored them.

- Calligraphy - it is enough to say that many times he couldn't decipher his own writing.

- Fluent speech - I found his vocabulary was very poor. Mostly because he didn't read. It also caused him problems with other subjects, like history or biology. He tended to use colloquial language all too often and he oversimplified his statements.

As you can see, it isn't rocket science. Those are a primary school student's problems. They are relatively easy to face. But first, I needed to recognize them and their scale. I was able to locate them by simply doing the homework with him for a couple of weeks.

Do the same. Find a bottom line, the source of your child's difficulties. It may be trouble with focus, with counting, with reading, lack of basic skills or knowledge. Whatever the reason is, find it. Only then can you help him/her effectively.

# Tactics

The particular tactics I used to overcome my son's problems may not be the ones you need to apply in the case of your child. I just want you to take a look at my approach and come up with your own tactics. Of course, if your kid has the exact difficulties as mine (for example, slow reading), those tactics are directly applicable for you, too.

## First and Foremost - Homework

I've already mentioned the first advantage of doing homework together in the previous chapter - recognizing the problem areas. But there are a lot more advantages than just that.

Nathaniel is smart, but lazy. Only a small part of his trouble came from a lack of knowledge or skill. Most of the times, he just didn't do his homework, because he had more interesting things to do (read: playing with his mates).

He was 10 years old; he wasn't a baby that needed watching every step. So we worked out the new procedure for doing homework: he did it after school, and when I came back from work, I marked it. Sometimes he would leave some difficult exercise undone, counting on my help (I almost cured him of this habit after several months of doing homework together). Then we worked on the problem areas, the things he couldn't understand. Later on, he was correcting the homework according to my suggestions. Lastly, I made the final revision.

That procedure puts the most work on his shoulders. All in all, it was his homework and his responsibility. On the other hand, I could focus on what's important - teaching when he couldn't grasp some concepts and on correcting mistakes.

There were days when it took us up to one hour, but there were days when we dealt with the homework within five minutes.

Doing homework together was also an excellent occasion to work on his writing (spelling and calligraphy), unobtrusively. It happened just by the way. Many times, I couldn't read what he wrote, and in such cases he was supposed to write the unreadable word in his calligraphy exercise book. And I was checking his spelling in the process.

I observed his carelessness in the way he did his lessons. He just wanted to get rid of the duty and go to the more fun activities. The quality of his work always suffered because of this attitude. The writing exercises were a great way to train his temper.

Gradually, he learned to do his homework slowly and carefully, focusing on the job, so he didn't have to repeat the process again and again correcting his writing and mistakes.

I want you to get the full importance of such a basic activity as doing homework together. Take a look of the list of advantages once again:

- gathering information about your kid's skills, knowledge, weak spots and mannerisms
- an occasion to work on basic skills, like spelling and calligraphy
- a way to learn self-discipline and consistency (for both of you)
- nipping the child's mistakes and misbehaviors in the bud and on the fly
- a chance to spend time together and strengthen your relationship (and we all know that rules without relationship is a recipe for rebellion, don't we?)

## Reading

I'm a firm believer of consistent and continuous practice. I also found that many of my son's difficulties come from his poor reading capability. He neglected this skill, he just did what was necessary to survive in a school environment and nothing more. I dread to think at what level are the reading skills of other kids from his class, the ones who got mostly "Cs", not "Bs".

Anyway, Nathaniel's vocabulary was poor. His spelling, storytelling and speaking abilities suffered because of that. His pronouncements were extremely clumsy for such a smart 10-year-old boy.

The remedy was simple - a daily reading assignment. At the beginning, he had to read just several pages a day, usually about five. As I mentioned in the second chapter, he read very slowly. Three years after learning reading, he still murmured while reading. In egghead's language, it's called sub-vocalization, and had a devastating impact on his reading speed.

Sub-vocalization, or silent speech, is defined as the internal speech made when reading a word, thus allowing the reader to imagine the sound of the word as it is read. This is a natural process when reading. Sub-vocalization is popularly associated with moving one's lips, the actual term refers primarily to the movement of muscles associated with speaking, not the literal moving of lips. Well, his silent speech wasn't so silent after all; he really moved his lips while reading.

So I introduced some basic speed reading techniques into his reading training. There are some advanced and difficult methods, but I made him use the simplest one first - biting his tongue and pursing his lips.

I gradually increased the scope of his assignments, but not very much. Every day, Nathaniel reads a chapter of a book, four to 12 pages. What is important, and what makes this simple task bring such great results, is consistency. He has read every single day since October 2012. Or almost every day - he tried to cheat by telling me he read that day, when he really didn't.

I understand him. He hated reading and he still doesn't enjoy it very much. It's normal; I also don't like to do things I'm not good at. But in modern society, an aversion to reading is as ridiculous as an aversion to breathing. So we needed to get past his moods. After several cases of "amnesia" regarding his reading assignment, I started to demand a report from the story. And you know what? That gave me an ideal chance to improve his storytelling. I listen to the stories told by him and I correct him on the fly. I show him how better wording could be used in this or that particular sentence. I make him wonder about the word's meaning.

In my book *Learn to Read with Great Speed*, I told the whole fascinating story of Nathaniel's reading adventure. Let me just state that there was a moment when he almost tripled his reading speed. He has also read all seven parts of *The Chronicles of Narnia*, and four other books during the training process. This is more than 70% of what adult Americans have read in 2012[1]. And it's just 10 months, in his case.

I give much credit for his overall improvement to this mundane task. He reads faster now, he understands more of what he reads and his vocabulary has expanded. It all had an impact on his other subjects, not just Polish. He can follow the references in math exercises now ;)

## English

We started learning English almost from scratch. Nathaniel had taken the line of least resistance in his English classes. He is just a genius at avoiding the work. So he found a way to hardly know English at all and still get good (well, not very bad) grades. My son learned the basics of basics. He knew the differences in phonetic spelling between English and Polish and a handful of words.

I'm no educationist. I don't know efficient techniques for teaching a foreign language. And I had no time to learn them. But I knew that consistently applied effort brings results. So the sole method I used was teaching him new English words. Of course, there were occasions to teach some grammar and rules while doing homework, but the foreign language program, as such, came down to mostly teaching new words.

---

1. http://libraries.pewinternet.org/2012/12/27/e-book-reading-jumps-print-book-reading-declines/

At the beginning, I made him write out about 30 words and he was learning them each day. When he tackled that material, I obligated him to write down and learn three new words a day. And I examined him almost every day. We took breaks from adding new words when I observed that it was too much for him to absorb. In such cases, he stopped adding new words for a few days and focused on learning those he had already written down before. I also made him memorize the forms of "to be" and "to have."

In order not to overwhelm him, we took breaks for holidays, too. During the summer holidays, he has to learn just one new word each day.

And that's it. He is still far away from being familiar with English, nothing to say about fluency, but he has many more skills regarding foreign language than he had before. He knows the difference between singular and plural, between first and third person. He can construct sentences, including negative and interrogative ones.

He took part in a school contest, without any success worth mentioning, but the participation alone was a success. It was an indicator that his teacher saw the improvement.

# Tips

You need to be consistent and demand performance from yourself. Never give up. You may have the impression that all my methods were implemented smoothly and without many difficulties. Well, they weren't.

## Consistency is the Key

Beware of the "everything is gonna be all right" feeling. It's not going to be all right, unless you make it all right. Consistency is a key factor that brings the results. I neglected the discipline of checking Nathaniel's progress about a dozen times, based on a false hope that he grasped it already, that he would continue on his own from now on. He didn't and he won't. It was my laziness and neediness of comfort which inspired those breaks, not the real effects of our work.

Every time I neglected this discipline, I observed my son slacking off almost immediately. When he knew I was going to ask him about the story he read, examine him on English words and so on, he had to be constantly prepared. But when he noticed I wasn't paying attention, he was more than happy to take care of other "business", defined as watching cartoons, playing with mates, playing the computer - instead of learning. He again took the line of least resistance.

If you are tired, exhausted and say to yourself, "I'll skip it, just this one time," remember that your child is more than eager to skip it one, two times and keep skipping it forever. That's why you started in the first place. It's your responsibility to keep going; the kid's cooperation is reluctant, at best.

It's not really **what** you are doing with your kid that matters, it's the consistency. My experience shows that you don't have to do **everything**, every time. The bottom line is to do something every day. So, when I was exhausted, I only examined Nathaniel's English vocabulary. Or I asked him about the story read today. Or I checked his homework.

Just remember to switch every so often between activities. Kids are amazingly adaptable and tend towards the line of least resistance. Nathaniel does not even do it purposefully. As I said before, during the summer holidays, he was obligated to read a chapter of a book and learn a single English word a day. But when he noticed I didn't check on his English words for a few days, or I didn't ask him to tell me today's story from a book, it immediately wasn't his priority. He postponed it for later in the day, and if I didn't remind him - he didn't do it that day at all.

## Put the Majority of the Work on Your Kid's Shoulders

My ultimate goal was to make my son's learning process more independent, so I wouldn't have to supervise him around the clock. And I think that's the goal of every sensible parent. We cannot be there for them to help and teach them for the rest of their lives. The purpose of all this fuss is to make them self-sufficient, isn't it? So I structured the learning program in a way that made him do most of the work. For example, during summer vacation he read for about 15 minutes, he studied English for several minutes and I examined him for a few minutes. He does 80% of the job alone and 20% with my help.

Remember - you are the one with the job to go to, bills to pay and all the other adult responsibilities. The majority of your work is simply to supervise. It's your son/daughter who has to do the major chunk of the job. Don't do his/her homework, don't read his/her books, don't bother yourself with details such as which exact new words should he/she learn now. Your child is perfectly capable of doing all those things.

Your goal is to improve the knowledge and skills of your kid. It's not going to happen if he/she doesn't stretch, doesn't grow. That's another reason to put most of the work on his/her shoulders. Of course, beware of overdoing, of putting too much on him/her – they are just kids, after all.

In addition, if you are as busy as I assume, you won't have time to supervise every assignment you put on him/her, if you give too many of them.

That's another advantage of the 10-minute philosophy, in the case of teaching children. It's just as much as you can do in such a short time span, so it's not likely you'll demand too much.

## Making the Learning Process Interesting

I don't know about you, but when I was a kid, I wasn't motivated by the perspective of good grades. Yeah, it was nice to get them, but it wasn't the prospect of getting an "A" which kept me in front of the books.

Anyone would go crazy after some time, if he had to work day after day on tasks he hates. Kids need diversity and something more than duty to keep their focus. That's why Nathaniel had to read not only the school lectures, but also *The Chronicles of Narnia*, which he found interesting. I did also give him some reading assignments from the *Encyclopedia of Animals*, because he loves all kinds of creatures. He hates reading anyway, but this task was a little more bearable for him when having something more engaging to read.

Don't make your child memorize everything the way it is taught in textbooks. I found language, even in the primary school textbooks, overly dry and cerebral. Try to explain the things your kid doesn't understand in simpler terms or by using life examples. I want my son to understand the material in a way he is capable of absorbing, not just to get better grades at school. And it's more effective, anyway. He just doesn't grasp any academic terms.

For example: hillock in his Natural Science textbook is defined as: "a terrain elevation having up to 50 meters of the relative altitude." And I said: "It's a small hill, sonny."

Try to introduce an element of play or challenge into the learning process. Your child is out of kindergarten, so there doesn't need to be a lot of play, but a pinch here and there can only help. Learning just for the sake of learning has a hypnotizing, numbing effect on the mind. I'm not good at playing while teaching, but I made a joke from time to time when discussing the story read today by my son. Or I used a funny example to illustrate my point, while explaining some natural science phenomena. Well, the best fun we had was when we tried to decipher his writing. We invented a lot of funny words then.

As to the challenges, I made it a contest between my sons a few times. They were examining each other's knowledge of English words. Including my older son made a family activity out of an otherwise mundane job. It also stirred up some excitement in Nathaniel. And the best of it? I was freed from examining him myself and I could do something else.

Even if you have only one child you can introduce the element of challenge. Your kid just needs to be challenged against himself/herself. Which brings me to the next tip: set goals, rewards and punishments. It worked perfectly in the case of reading practice with my son. I set a specific word-per-minute goal for him to achieve by the end of each month of practice. If he succeeded, he did reap a reward we both agreed upon - more time to play outside, more time to play on the computer and so forth. If he failed, he got something less pleasurable, like additional household duties. Again, we discussed the punishment in advance and we both agreed on it.

I set goals which made him stretch, struggle. On the 18th of October, he read 71 words per minute. By the end of the month, I wanted him to read 100 wpm. He did it and he got ungrounded. Then I set him a 130 wpm limit for the end of November. He succeeded again and was allowed more time to play on the computer and, most importantly, he was happy about himself, because he achieved something extraordinary - at least for him. We made a different arrangement for December, as it was the month of winter holidays: he just had to keep his reading speed of 130 wpm. We agreed on no reward, but he would get a punishment if he slacked off.

Just keep in mind that you must be prepared for both eventual reward and punishment. Don't agree on five additional hours on the computer or your kid won't have time for doing homework. And if you plan some sanction, make sure you are willing and able to enforce it.

I made an agreement with Nathaniel for a particular month, that if he didn't reach the specific words-per-minute limit, he would have to play with his younger sister every day for the next month. He failed to accomplish it and I had an additional duty - keeping watch on his new obligation.

## Follow the Kid's New Lessons

Don't restrict yourself to his/her current homework. It's also helpful to ask your child what new information he/she has learned today and check if he/she understood the new material. In Poland, this task is easier for a parent, as kids carry their textbooks in their backpack all the time. I just needed to go through Nathaniel's backpack every day, take all his textbooks out and have him show me his last lesson. Then I skipped through it, asked him a few questions and immediately I knew which part he grasped and which he didn't. And it was an additional opportunity to correct his speaking manners and vocabulary.

Your child can have a backlog of knowledge to catch up on, but it is important that he/she can keep up the pace with ongoing material, too. It will make your life easier in the long run. You won't have to play catch-up forever, but just to the point at which you started.

## It's Hard to Start,
## but it's Easy to Keep Momentum Going

The setup of our teaching sessions was a nightmare. For the first couple of weeks, it took me about an hour a day to go through various activities - check new lessons, mark the homework, examining English words and more. I needed to tame a "wild beast" - my son was not used to regular practice sessions. At all.

Be very careful in this initial period. Do not deplete your motivation too fast. Keep in mind that it's just temporary. Once you implement the teaching process and make a habit of it both for your kid and for you, it will get easier. As Johann Wolfgang von Goethe said: "Everything is hard before it's easy".

You can read more about willpower and motivation depletion on a very interesting blog about habit development: www.developgoodhabits.com

Anyway, it **really** gets easier after some time. You and your child will be more proficient in your tasks. Then, you start to win over his/her problems one by one. The backlog will decrease. Step by step, you will move forward and time commitment will decrease, too.

After the initial period of intense work, I restricted some activities, like going through Nathaniel's backpack (and new lessons) to about once, twice a week. After a couple of months of calligraphy exercises, he became more careful and he wrote a little better. I became more accustomed to his writing style. I could finally read what he wrote ;) And we stopped those exercises altogether.

He didn't get homework every day, so we were free from this activity every second, third day. Gradually, more often than not, the teaching tasks took me 10 minutes or less. Then we could schedule some bigger chunks of the teaching program for weekends, when I had more time for him.

It only looked overwhelming at the beginning. All in all, those were just a primary school student's problems. They are easy to deal with by an adult!

## Be a Good Example

It's almost the last tip, but not the least important. Integrity is not something you can lecture into your child. You have to show it. You don't just show him/her that you care, you **must** actually care, to be able to show it.

I repeat to my son, time after time, the sentence: "Your duties go first; your pleasures go second." That's the rule I want to instill in him for the rest of his life. And as soon as I don't practice what I preach, he goes for his pleasures first. Especially if the duty in question is our teaching program. Every time I neglected my commitment in the process, his commitment dropped rapidly, too.

I don't know if you are familiar with *The 7 Habits of Highly Effective People*. Its author, Stephen R. Covey, explains the concept of the Circle of Influence as "the things you can do something about" against the concept of the Circle of Concern - things you are worried about, but have no real control over, like global warming or the national debt.

It's easy to mistake those circles in the case of teaching your child. Trust me, I know something about it. You probably assume - like almost everybody - that the homework of your kid is in your circle of influence.

Wrong!

You can't do his/her homework. It's your child's job. You can force your kid to do the homework once, twice, several times, but the expenditure of power is so much greater than the results you get. So, you must seek to find things you can do something about. Your job is to focus on them. I found that out the hard way and I share it, so you won't repeat my mistakes.

I discovered that Nathaniel's homework concerns me, but I can't actually do it for him or with him. I found I can do other things - check on him every day, remind him about the homework, mark it if done. That was (and still is) my responsibility.

Don't repeat my mistakes. Keep in mind that you are an adult, a leader in this partnership and it's your responsibility to keep the momentum going. The best way to deal with it, is to make a habit out of it - an automatic activity you don't have to ponder much upon. And remember: focus on the things you can do something about.

## Triggers and Tracking

Schedule a block of time for each day. I would suggest at least an hour for the initial week. If it takes less time - fine. Rephrasing the old saying - it's better to reserve too much time and not need it than to reserve too little and not have enough.

A very useful tool for habit creation is a trigger. If you have any common ritual already established with your child - cleaning the room after school, watching a favorite cartoon together - use it as an introduction to a teaching session. If your daily schedule is reasonably routine, it's easier. The ideal solution is to schedule this block of time at the same hour every day.

However, the world we live in is not ideal. My schedule is hectic. I work different shifts, sometimes overtime at night, and I need to sleep during the day, so regular hours for my work with Nathaniel are out of the question. What helped me to keep a consistency was a tracking system, the most basic of all imaginable - pen and paper.

I already track some of my daily activities this way. I prepare a piece of paper, write the names of activities in the first column, the days of the week or month in the columns' header and check them off when I fulfill a specific obligation. I just added "Nathaniel's lessons" into the system. Whenever I found an empty field in my chart or a minus sign - which means I caught myself neglecting the lesson on a given day - I knew I needed to pay extra attention to his lessons, because it was me who slacked off this time.

I encourage you to imitate my system, because it is really simple and it takes virtually no time to use - unless of course, you already have a tracking system of your own. If you use a different tool for similar purposes, like an application on your mobile to check off your to-do tasks, then just incorporate tracking the teaching sessions into it.

You may have other ideas on how to achieve a daily consistency more suitable for you and your child's temperament. For example, you could track together all the partial activities on the big board put on the wall in his/her room - reading, English, homework etc. Put happy or sad faces in the chart's cells. Make it fun and interesting for your kid to participate in tracking. Attach a system of rewards/penalties to it.

Do it your way. Use the method which is best suited for you to make a habit of the daily teaching session. Just keep in mind the two bottom-line parameters of your tracking system - it must be fast and it must be easy to use.

You are a terribly busy parent, aren't you? So don't make the mistake of creating an overly complicated tracking tool. Let's say you picked an Evernote to track your daily "lessons," but you don't usually use it. Each time after your session with son/daughter, you turn on your old stationary computer, wait for the system to launch, put the password to log in, connect to the Internet, give your credentials to the Evernote app and fill the proper fields in it. Then you still have to turn off your computer.

Do you get the picture? Such an approach is totally missing the point of a tracking system!

If you miss the lesson, you must be able to catch yourself at it. That's why your tracking method must be habitual and easy to use.

.

# Conclusion

This book, *Release Your Kid's Dormant Genius,* is not a textbook. I put my personal story in it, the insights into my family life, with one sole, single-minded purpose: to inspire you. If you see your child in trouble, if you feel helpless and don't know what to do, I've just given you a formula. Start. Persevere. Fine tune your methods. And do it until it works. Every sustained action brings results.

It's possible to change your child's future. It's doable, even if you have only 10 minutes a day. Even if you have neglected his/her education until now (that was what I did, I left Nathaniel's education in the hands of his teachers).

Kids need only a little encouragement, guidance, attention. Just be there.

Hey, if you are disappointed with my advice and my story, because you are doing much more for your kid, you are just a much better parent than me, take a look at it from another perspective: if such a poor excuse of a father as Michal could achieve so much, then what could YOU achieve?

If that thought inspires you to increase your efforts, I'm

totally comfortable and happy with it.

I would appreciate you sending me an email with the news when you achieve something worth mentioning in your opinion - for example some progress of your child's education. I just want to know that my work helped one more person.

A simple message to **parent@onedollartips.com** will be enough, although any other feedback is much welcomed, too. I'm also interested in some unique ways you've come up with to implement your individual educational program.

Take care. I don't wish you luck. I wish you the desire to change your kid's destiny and personal satisfaction, and to know that it was you who helped in making it possible.

Don't miss the full story of Nathaniel's struggles in the next chapter.

# Nathaniel's Story

To put it simply, Nathaniel hasn't a scholar's inclinations. He is very active, he likes sports, he loves to play outside with other children. He has very little interest in books, he would much rather watch movies.

The first three grades of primary school weren't a problem for him. He is a bright guy. He could read even before he started school. He is a kind of math genius. As an 8-year-old, he could multiply two-digit numbers in memory.

We noticed his tendency to slack off, but he was always able to catch up. It was disturbing, but not alarming. He was generally a "B" level student. He was smarter than that and he often got "As", but he occasionally got "Cs" and even some "Ds", too.

But the brightness and talent could bring him only so far. The problems began for him in the 4th grade.

In Poland, the shift between 3rd and 4th grade is quite radical. The first three grades are a kind of school incubator. Children learn just a few subjects - math, Polish, English, basics of natural science, PE and art. 80% of classes are conducted by one teacher who is responsible for a particular class. If a child is on good terms with this teacher, his/her life is much easier. And my son has a lot of personal charm.

The 4th grade is a whole different story. Several new subjects are introduced. There is a different teacher for each subject. Pupils have to move around the school from one lesson to another. But those are just additional distractions. The main shift is that kids really need to start comprehending what they are taught.

And it is a lot of effort for a 10-year-old kid who didn't have to try to learn very hard in the past.

Nathaniel did what we do unconsciously when we are given the choice - he took the easy way. He didn't learn, he didn't read, he did his homework only when it was necessary - well, not even so often. He used every possible excuse facing his teachers.

In Poland, the primary school pupil is allowed to be unprepared for a lesson - may have no homework done, have no idea how to answer the question from the last lesson - twice per semester. It is a privilege reserved for extraordinary situations - the child was on a trip with family, sickness, something important had happened and the kid forgot or was unable to fulfill his obligations.

Nathaniel used almost all his "unpreparations" within the first seven weeks of the semester. He also got some negative grades because of lack of homework or lack of knowledge. But the worst of it was that he lied to us. When asked about homework, he had been saying - with a poker face - there was none or he did it flawlessly. He pretended that everything was all right. He made it to the last possible moment - when I was going to the first parent teacher meeting I told him it was his final chance to confess his actual school sins. "Everything is all right," he lied.

Half an hour later, I discovered that it wasn't.

We had a very turbulent evening that night. Nathaniel got grounded. I decided that we needed more control over his learning process. I started going through his backpack (and new lessons) almost every day. Whenever I found homework to do or already done, we either did it together or I marked it. As you know from previous chapters, I quickly identified his weak spots and started a few disciplines to neutralize them. Reading, memorizing English words, spelling, calligraphy and so on.

The first breakthrough came just two weeks later. I set him the goal of reading 100 words per minute by the end of the month. I didn't really believe he was capable of such progress (it's an over 40% increase) and neither did he. But - surprise, surprise - sustained action brings results. He was reading several pages a day for 13 days and it made all the difference.

It was a blessing. The first weeks were very tense. He was ashamed of himself, we were angry at him and the initial effort of implementing our teaching program was tiresome for both of us.

Nathaniel hated reading. I had to almost sit on him to make him read. Suddenly, he discovered he could improve by a simple daily practice. His attitude changed a bit. He was looking forward to the next reading exam, being confident that he was able to cope with it and to get the reward. I could ease up a little on reading and place my attention on other areas of his education.

Then another effect of our program became visible - his grades improved almost immediately. He is smart, he just needed to put some more effort into the learning process. He did it and he reaped the fruits of his labors.

I set him a 130 wpm reading goal for the end of

November. He succeeded again, so he was allowed more time to play on the computer and most importantly, he was happy about himself, because he achieved something extraordinary: an 83% improvement in reading speed within six weeks. His confidence in himself grew.

Then came December, the month of winter holidays and Nathaniel was doing well, so I let go the pressure a little. My mistake.

I eased up on me. I had more time for different activities. And my son took advantage of it. In January, I was at another, not very optimistic, parent-teacher meeting. But his situation still was much better than in October. He was at risk of a "C" in only two subjects, and he generally achieved his solid "B" level as during the first three grades.

At the end of the first semester, he had to make up for some lessons and he only got a "C" in Natural Science. That was far better than October's gloomy predictions.

We continued our program with its ups and downs. I tell you, his results were directly proportional to the effort I was willing to put into teaching. When I eased up just a little, so did he. When I put in more time and commitment, he did, too.

From January to April, he was in a "frustration period." First of all, he didn't understand why he had to learn and practice skills daily. He was satisfied with his previous level at school and was content, so what was the reason of further "torment?" Second, his progress in reading came to a standstill. He had read 120-130 words per minute since the beginning of December and he couldn't improve. This lack of result discouraged him a lot and the only power which kept him at reading practices was my determination. For several weeks, we established the ritual, the contest of will. When I got home from work, I would ask him, "Have you read today?"

"Not yet" - was his standard answer.

"Then do so." - and he did comply, grudgingly.

Needless to say, if I forgot to ask, he "forgot to read" that day.

To discourage him further, another disaster came. He was sick for a week and he forgot to ask a schoolmate about math homework. He didn't know about it, so he didn't do it. He got four or five "Fs because of it. And it was math, his favorite subject! The splendor of education was not something he could appreciate then.

During that period, we met with a pedagogue and psychologist a few times to determine if he was dyslexic. They said he was too young to determine that with certainty, but they saw he had some troubles with writing and spelling. They also estimated his IQ level as above average and ascertained he had extraordinary math skills. They advised to practice reading and spelling to improve his weak spots.

And we practiced.

Another breakthrough was involved with reading, too. In the middle of April, we were preparing for another reading test, when I proposed:

"Use your finger as a pointer." - this is another basic speed reading technique, but I had never mentioned it to him before. I had been focusing on eliminating his excessive sub-vocalization.

"OK" - he agreed hesitantly. He had never done it before.

BAM! His result was 170 words per minute!

It gave both of us motivation to continue, to keep our efforts going. At the end of June, he achieved 192 words per minute, his life record up to then.

As usual, after the success came a failure. Nathaniel was so confident in his skill that he neglected his practice. And I was foolish enough to leave it in his hands. His results declined and we came back to the same old routine. I started to examine him from the text he had read on a daily basis, and I found it a good time to correct his speech mannerisms.

Another parent-teacher meeting wasn't very encouraging. Admittedly he had more "As" than "Bs", but he added some more "Cs" and "Ds" to the collection. The worst situation was in regard to Natural Science - "C" for the first semester and only one "C" and one "D" this semester. We had less than two months to fix it.

I snapped out of complacency and got to work. Still about 5-20 minutes a day. I just didn't have more time. But our activities were well rehearsed from times past. I just put more attention on our teaching program, and Nathaniel noticed that I was more serious and he got the message. Nothing fancy, nothing new, just consistency.

The only addition to our program was a short (just a few minutes long) Natural Science rehearsal session twice a week. He was supposed to learn it every day.

I don't have any idea how Nathaniel did it, but he set his marks right for the Natural Science class, as well as a bunch of other subjects. He finished the school year with honors! He got a "B" in Natural Science and English. The rest were "As"!

He also got the motivation to learn better in the next school year. My other son, Christopher, had a better average than him and he got a "scholarship," more of an award than a scholarship – thirty bucks given solemnly by the school director. However, the bucks had much more to do with this motivation than solemnity. ;)

That should constitute the happy end of his story, but life goes on ... I eased up on him again. It was the summer holiday after all! But the June's reading test revealed a drastic decrease in his reading speed, so for the past two months, I have made sure that he reads every day. He has read two more books, about 300 pages. I saw also to adding a new English word to his vocabulary every day.

The new school year is coming. I'm steeling myself to continue our teaching program. Nathaniel wants to get a scholarship - at least he says so. We will see.

## Update

I wrote the book during the summer holiday of 2013 and, subsequently, Nathaniel slacked off once again.

October's parent-teacher meeting wasn't much better than the previous year. But still ... a little better.

He got grounded again. But he fixed his marks almost instantly this time. At the beginning of December, it seems that he is going to get only three "Bs" at the end of the semester. And knowing his magic ability to improve the grades at the last possible moment, maybe he will even exceed those expectations.

# MASTER Your TIME

## IN 10 MINUTES A DAY

### TIME MANAGEMENT TIPS FOR ANYONE STRUGGLING WITH WORK – LIFE BALANCE

# Introduction

*"Time is what we want most, but what we use worst."*
## - **William Penn**

I won't bore you to death by preaching about the importance of time management, about how time is your most precious commodity and cannot be bought or reclaimed, about how we all have the same amount of it, or how the thing setting us apart is how we make use of it and blah, blah, blah.

Enough has already been written about that, by visionaries and eggheads alike. I do not need to reaffirm the importance of your own life, your own time. Chances are, if you are reading this book, your life and time are already of great value to you.

Whatever your goal may be, I assume you are not in the position to drop everything else and commit all your resources - especially your time - to fulfilling it. Your life is an ongoing project, not something to make from scratch starting today.

Theoretical ruminations have their place, but this book will not be one. Since you are committing some of your valuable time to read this book, you likely have some questions:

- does the author of this book know more about time management than I do?
- how effectively does he use his time? Is he a person I can follow?
- is his advice applicable in my situation?

These are good questions to be asking; they show that you put energy into determining if something is worth your time. Well, fear not.

I think you can relate to me. I'm what you might consider an ordinary person, not an ivory tower guru. I commute, work a 9 to 5 job, have a family and attend church regularly.

As far as my qualifications go, I will leave you to draw your own conclusions. I don't know you or how much you can squeeze into 24 hours, but have a look at my typical day and compare it to your own:

- I'm a full time employee and my total daily commute adds about three and half hours to each workday.
- I know the importance of sleep to one's overall state of being, so I try very hard to sleep at least seven hours a day (which usually means I get six and a half).
- Every day for me also includes 20 minutes of prayer, 60-90 minutes of writing and at least 30 minutes of reading.
- Additionally, I spend about 15 minutes on meditation and self-analysis every morning.
- I exercise 20 to 30 minutes per day and listen to

educational and/or motivational materials for 20 minutes.

- Every day, I review my 1,300-word personal mission statement. I study the Bible, read professional literature and practice speed reading, each for about 10 minutes per day.

- I keep three different gratitude journals - one about my wife, one about my kids and one about my life as a whole. I have a very personal blog, (another journal, really) and I post there daily, taking another 5-10 minutes.

- I'm involved in a few online communities on a daily basis, and I learn about writing, publishing and marketing by following a few blogs.

If you have been doing the mental math, you've seen that my daily commitments (sleep included) add up to at least 23 hours of each day. Yes, I do still find time to breathe.

To track my progress and dedication to my daily tasks, check me out here:
**https://www.coach.me/users/360e9cc8df81879e1935**

Many people set goals to build new habits, but then abandon them too quickly. The power of daily habits, if sustained, is immense.

I wrote about 150,000 words in 2013 - just for my blogs, short stories and books. I've read more than 40 books and hundreds of blog posts. I have a whole notepad full of the self-knowledge I've gained - my goals, plans, desires, motivations, obstacles, dreams, doubts and beliefs.

In addition to the tasks I complete every day, I also have other weekly, monthly and irregular commitments.

For more than 16 years, I have been an active member of my church community. This adds three to five hours of commitments weekly. Additionally, every month I take the time to make a financial statement for the past month and budget estimation for the next.

You might think, with all of those regular commitments, I would be tapped out at the end of each day. But, as you will see, my productivity doesn't end there.

In addition to all my daily tasks, I've launched three WordPress sites since the beginning of 2013 - a personal blog, a blog for me as an author, and also a project that's a little harder to define. I manage all three sites on my own.

First, I had to learn how to create and manage WordPress sites. Then it was off to learn how to buy a domain and hosting, how to merge different domains onto one hosting platform, how to remove spam comments, how to install and manage plugins, updates and widgets. I had to discover how to make sense of my website analytics.

And the list goes on.

I've made a lot of personal development materials for my own use. I've recorded several hours of audio and rewritten the book, *The Science of Getting Rich*, in its entirety to make it more congruent with my faith and values.

I overcame my shyness. I talk with strangers from time to time and always send a smile their way.

I published five Kindle books in 2013. That process involves so much more than just writing - research, cover design, formatting, marketing, payment, and tax issues.

And the list goes on.

I have a couple of other projects which haven't seen the sunlight yet.

I've even found time to devote to my hobbies; in August 2013, I organized and participated in a collectable card game tournament.

Last, but certainly not least, I've been married since 2000 and I have three kids. My family is important to me and I give them as much of my time and attention as I can: dates with my wife, games with my kids, reading to my daughter, doing homework with my boys. Walks, chats, going to the circus, cinema, theatre or swimming pool.

I also found time to take a two-week vacation. While on vacation, I took a complete break from working and writing. It was enjoyable and refreshing.

I didn't share this background with you just to impress you. I wrote all of this because I imagine that you can relate. Take a moment to compare your story with mine. If it sounds similar and you want to learn my productivity concepts, then this book is for you.

If you have more obligations and projects, if you find that you are already more productive, reading this book might not be an effective use of your time. My goal is to serve you, not disadvantage you, so if that's the case - skip this book.

I want to show you how to extract more value from your time and find more fulfilment in your life. So, if you are now curious how I do all this and reconcile it with a full time job - read on.

This book has recently gotten a few negative comments with one common theme: "Nothing new here." All I have to say in reply is: This is a book about mastering your time, not about fashion. If you're looking for novelty, look somewhere else!

## Action Items

**Read the introduction and make four lists (actually write these down):**

- Daily Obligations
- Weekly Obligations
- Monthly and Irregular Obligations
- Goals

Compare our lists and see if your time constraints and aspirations look similar to mine.

**If you feel you stand to benefit by reading my methods of time management, read on!**

# Motivation

*"Until you value yourself, you won't value your time.*
*Until you value your time, you will not do anything with it."*

## - M. Scott Peck

If you can answer at any given time, to any given person, without hesitation, the question, "What's your purpose in life?" you can go ahead and skip this chapter. If not, I urge you to read it closely. Your purpose must be the driving force behind improving your time management. Without a reason to do so, working on your time-management skills will not bring meaningful results.

Tips and techniques are great tools to have, but all the knowledge in the world will do you no good if you won't implement it. You need a purpose to do anything in life, managing your time included. That reason must be big enough to overcome the inertia, bigger than the multitude of reasons to take a break, to let go.

Time management starts in your head. Your mind is the true source of your procrastination. But, it's also the true source of your productivity. The cynic or hardcore realist might find it hard to believe, but it is **the truth**.

Nothing exists without first being created, and in your life, **that creation begins in your mind**.

Here is how the motivation story played out for me: I read *Getting Things Done* by David Allen in November 2011. Allen's book contains the most brilliant time management system I have ever seen. Everything is explained very clearly and arranged methodically. The system's simplicity and reported effectiveness led me to try it.

So, I tried and tried and tried ...

Trying was all I could achieve without the internal motivation. Don't get me wrong, every tip and technique, if used correctly, is fruitful. Even just **trying** Mr. Allen's methods **haphazardly** helped me manage my time better. But, by developing the motivation to **stand firmly behind** each technique, I began to see results that were greater by orders of magnitude!

Just think of someone doing his job because he is truly passionate about that work. Perhaps you have a coworker or friend who has that zeal for their work. Then think of someone who works just to get by. They may even do all of the same actions, after all it is the same job. But, the results they achieve and the amount of effort they both put in to achieve those results, are very different. Find just two examples from your experience and contemplate the differences.

In August 2012, I read another book that enabled me to manage my time even better than *Getting Things Done*. It wasn't a time management book at all; it was a personal development book titled *The Slight Edge* by Jeff Olson. This book drove me to seek meaningful change in my life. The self-improvement I worked on as a result, led to the development of an **impassioned motivation**, different from anything I had ever felt before. This new vigor gave me the ability to extract **far more value** from my time than ever before.

That's why I encourage you to search for your reasons first and, only then, apply these new time management techniques.

Why do you want to save time? Why do you want to be more effective? Why do you want to improve your productivity? What is the purpose behind those desires?

Forget wishes – they won't sustain you long enough to implement the techniques and build a new lifestyle.

## Find Your Purpose

Stephen R. Covey became a household name and multi-millionaire through the pursuit of his passion for helping others grow. He began his greatest work - *The 7 Habits of Highly Effective People*, the bible of effectiveness - with a search for self-awareness and personal values. The secret is more spiritual than technical, isn't it?

I complied with his advice and doing so enhanced my effectiveness significantly. One of the first steps I took in transforming my life was to formulate my **personal mission statement**. It took me over a month of writing and rewriting, but it was worth every second. I advise you to do the very same thing.

Think of it as your greatest investment in your time management program, quite possibly your life. Your personal mission statement is THE key to improving your time management a thousand-fold. Why waste your time on minor tasks when you can invest a few weeks to skyrocket your awareness and motivation?

Lasting change must start from the level of principles and values. With this approach, you can do the (seemingly) impossible. This is how I've developed lasting and productive habits.

As of right now (October 2013), I track 33 habits on Coach.me. A year ago, I tracked just two. And I have a few more which have become so automatic that I don't need to track them anymore. Additionally, I have a few weekly and monthly habits that are also new. Overall, I've developed about 40 new habits in the last year.

Now, to the point: In 10 minutes on Google, I found countless links to pages with advice on creating or changing habits. All of them are compatible: start easy, start slowly; don't try to revolutionize your life.

- http://www.self-improvement-mentor.com: "Changing a habit is one of the most difficult tasks that a person can undertake."
- PsyBlog: "The classic mistake people make (...) is to bite off more than they can chew."
- Leo Babauta: "(...) too many changes at once. I've seen that fail many times. (...) One habit change at a time. Some people can do two (...) and actually stick to it, but that's much more difficult. Once you get good at that, maybe you can do two at a time."
  By "at a time," Mr. Babauta means 4-6 weeks of implementation. If diligent, it is possible to create 13 new, lasting habits in one year.

I didn't know that advice going in, so I did it my way and implemented over three times as many habits. And I got rid of several that consumed far too much time, like playing computer games or watching TV.

In case you didn't notice, 24 hours do not seem like enough to do all of my daily habits and have a life. But I still manage to do it, something I attribute solely to the power contained in my personal mission statement, my internal drive.

There are three elements of behavioral change in BJ Fogg's Behavior Model: Motivation, Ability and Trigger. According to the model, motivation and ability are interchangeable. So, if you have low motivation but high ability, you can still succeed with your change. And vice versa - if you don't know how to introduce a change, but your motivation is high, you will find a way to succeed.

Finally, I had found something to explain my success: I have enormously high motivation (found through developing my mission statement). My abilities probably pale in comparison to the abilities of many people out there, and yet I have become more effective and successful than ever before!

If you don't buy the 'feelings approach,' then refer to the science. Do you want to manage your time efficiently, but don't know how? Then your Ability factor, in this area, is low and you need ... that's right, a high motivation. Again, this is where a personal mission statement can clarify what things drive you and help you to develop a new sense of motivation.

Define your life's purpose and your path to success will become evident. I've done many different things, for many different reasons, but I found there is no motivation like that which came with the realization of my life's purpose.

If you haven't already, I recommend that you read the first two chapters of *The 7 Habits of Highly Effective People* and write your personal mission statement.

If you want to save some money, you can buy my book *A Personal Mission Statement: Your Roadmap to Happiness* - just $1[1]; look for it on Amazon - and learn how to compose one. Or, if you have a lot of time for research, you can figure out it on your own; browse the Web and you will find volumes of advice about the process.

The action-oriented may see this step as a waste of time, but I assure you that action without contemplation is the true waste of time. Why? Because only sustained action brings lasting results. Without a purpose, sooner or later you will give up, even if you are – like me – extremely stubborn.

An example: I have been doing push-ups every day for half my life. Before I found a good enough reason, I started and abandoned this habit more times than I like to count. It took me about a decade to figure it out. My stubbornness was enough to keep me going for a year or two at a time, but it's the internal sense of purpose that has kept me going consistently for the last six years.

Your mindset is the foundation of your 'personal house.' But walls and roof, without a foundation, is only a tent, which probably won't withstand heavy rain or high winds.

---

## Action Items

- Create your own personal mission statement or use any alternative method which will help you to answer the question, "What is your purpose in life?"
- If you are an action-oriented, down-to-earth type of person, study BJ Fogg's Behavior Model first.

---

1. On the US market. On other markets additional fees or taxes may be applied.

# The Ultimate
# Time Management Tool

*"The bad news is time flies. The good news is you're the pilot."*
— **Michael Altshuler**

As I pointed out in the previous chapter, time management starts in your head. You need to work on your mindset to see any significant results. Don't worry, I won't force you to murmur the mantra: "I will do everything the most efficient way every minute, every day ..." ten times a day.

I believe affirmation can be a top-shelf tool for achieving results. I also believe, though, that it is a tool that requires mastery to produce significant results. Anyone can repeat mantras, but getting real life results from doing this is an art I certainly haven't mastered.

The tool I'm talking about is much simpler. You need just two skills to use it; skills you have had since childhood. All that this tool requires is that you are able to write and tell the time.

The ultimate tool I am referring to is the **time journal**.

The time journal works so amazingly well because of **its effectiveness and its simplicity**. Anybody can use it.

You may be thinking, "Oh, gimme a break; I know all about the time journal!"

I'll deal with this attitude a little further on. But if the idea is new to you, pay attention. A time journal is just a journal in which you write all your activities and how much time they take. The more specific you are about the kind of activity you've done and about the amount of time it took, the better it will work.

The minimum recommended by Jim Rohn is at least one entry in the time journal every 30 minutes. You can note time spans or mark the beginning and end of activities. Some schools of thought also suggest that you write down your moods and distractions.

Choose the method most suitable for you. If you carry a smartphone, there are plenty of time tracking apps can help you. Or you can simply use a pen and paper. Just pick your golden rule, whatever is most convenient for you and stick with it.

I decided to start keeping a time journal, so I wrote down every activity I found myself doing and marked the start and stop times. I spend half of my life in front of a computer, so I used Excel to keep all of these entries. If I was away from the computer, I would jot things down in a pocket notepad and enter them in my spreadsheet as soon as I returned to the computer.

To get a picture of what I'm talking about, take a peek into the beginning of my day on July 4, 2013:

| | begin time | end time | Activity | time span |
|---|---|---|---|---|
| 1 | begin time | end time | Activity | time span |
| 2 | 22:05 | 4:55 | sleep | 6:50 |
| 3 | 4:55 | 5:03 | bathroom, drink water, medicate nose | 0:08 |
| 4 | 5:03 | 5:17 | workout, listen to audio materials | 0:14 |
| 5 | 5:17 | 5:23 | brush teeth, listen to audio materials | 0:06 |
| 6 | 5:23 | 5:32 | prepare for work | 0:09 |
| 7 | 5:32 | 5:37 | excercise - dips | 0:05 |
| 8 | 5:37 | 5:41 | prepare for work | 0:04 |
| 9 | 5:41 | 5:48 | walk to train, prayer | 0:07 |
| 10 | 5:48 | 5:51 | read my philosophy notes | 0:03 |
| 11 | 5:51 | 5:57 | self-analysis exercise | 0:06 |
| 12 | 5:57 | 6:01 | time tracking | 0:04 |
| 13 | 6:01 | 6:52 | write 550 words | 0:51 |
| 14 | 6:52 | 6:58 | walk to bus, listen to my personal mission statement | 0:06 |
| 15 | 6:58 | 7:25 | bus ride, speed reading exercise | 0:27 |
| 16 | 7:25 | 7:30 | walk to the office, listen to my personal mission statement | 0:05 |
| 17 | 7:30 | 7:34 | prepare for work and time tracking | 0:04 |
| 18 | 7:34 | 7:41 | work related tasks | 0:07 |
| 19 | 7:41 | 8:03 | self-analysis exercise | 0:22 |
| 20 | 8:03 | 8:33 | write | 0:30 |
| 21 | 8:33 | 8:40 | breakfast - had watermelon | 0:07 |

You don't have to write down every detail. Again, for this to become a sustained habit, you need to do it in a way that works for you.

I used abbreviations for common activities to make the process faster.

What you see above is the version translated to common language, to make it understandable. The start time of an activity is taken automatically from the end time of the previous activity by an Excel formula.

Another formula calculates the activity's time span. It saved me time over inputting this manually.

See the "time tracking" entries?

Those are the points when I turned on the computer on a train and at the office (5:57 and 7:30 respectively) and rewrote the entries from my pocket notepad into an Excel sheet. After 7:34, I hardly needed any time dedicated solely to time tracking, as it was just a matter of changing the window on the computer, marking the time and jotting down an activity name.

Feel free to download and use my template:
**www.expandbeyondyourself.com/tools/time_journal_template.xls**

Remember to manually input sleep time in the first cell!

Some people, like successful serial entrepreneur Rich Schefren of Strategic Profits, merge their version of the time journal into their everyday activities and it becomes second nature for them. I recommend strict use of a detailed version (as presented in the fragment of my journal) for just two weeks. Repeat the exercise every few months to keep your level of awareness high.

If you have any reservations about keeping a time journal, think it over. Yes, it can be a little pesky to exercise such control over your day. Yes, it's a little strange to do and can make you feel like a weirdo, but are there really any other disadvantages to paying such close attention to where your time goes? None come to mind for me and I promise you **the advantages are much greater**.

This is your first step in building a more productive mindset. By keeping a time journal, you make yourself **aware** of how you spend your time. If you are interested in implementing a new time management strategy, it's likely because you don't use your time optimally. The time journal allows you to get to **the core of the problem**, to very clearly see areas where you are wasting time.

That's the main purpose of using this tool - to make you aware of how you really use your time. You can't improve if you don't know your starting position. **Most people believe they already know precisely how they use their time. Most people are wrong.**

There are dangers you should be aware of that come with keeping a time journal. By being conscious about tracking your time, you may find yourself changing your behavior just to make a more impressive journal. For a couple of weeks, you might limit your unproductive activities and then, as soon as you finish the tracking exercise, slip back into old, less effective habits.

Modern technology gives us tools that can help. If you spend a lot of time on the computer and using mobile devices, I recommend the RescueTime application. It runs in the background, gathering information about how you are spending your time. You can install it, forget about it and check back a week, or a month later.

**Knowledge, awareness and progress tracking are keys to making any improvement.** If you rush blindly into a venture just hoping everything will be all right, you are asking for trouble. If you do not first recognize where you are starting from, and don't measure your progress, you are setting yourself up to fail.

Be serious about keeping your time journal.

If you have never successfully done this, have never tried, or tried and gave up, this is a must-do.

Don't spend time preoccupied with what method you use to track your time – that's not the point. The point is - whatever system you implement - that you will become very aware of your baseline productivity. You'll see it improve before your eyes.

Drop the excuses and do it!

It is simple, it's easy, it works.

The big shots - Darren Hardy, Jim Rohn, Rich Schefren - have all used this technique and they all recommend it as a powerful productivity tool.

## Action Items

- Choose the most suitable form of recording your time journal.
- Keep a detailed time journal for two weeks.
- Use RescueTime for two weeks after this and check to see if you have slipped into any old habits.
- Use the time journal for two weeks every quarter.

# Work on What's Important
# Not What's Urgent

*"Most of us spend too much time on what is urgent
and not enough time on what is important."*

— **Stephen R. Covey**

If you've studied time management in any depth, you probably know the important/urgent activity matrix. If not, then check out this witty summary.

https://sidsavara.com/coveys-time-management-matrix-illustrated/

|  | Urgent | Not Urgent |
|---|---|---|
| **Important** | 1 | 2 |
| **Not Important** | 3 | 4 |

You must work on important projects to be effective. Again, it's a matter of your priorities. If you don't know the source of your motivation, you will tend to drift in the direction of other people's agendas. You will spend your time working on 'emergencies,' instead of on what's really important to you.

You may be very efficient in dealing with urgent issues, but still not be effective in the end - the proverbial "spinning your wheels." It may be appreciated at your job; it even may be crucial to your career (for example, if you are a doctor in emergency services). But it's highly unlikely to create the life of your dreams in the long run. Even a fireman's job doesn't consist solely of emergencies. There are long hours of training and supplementary education, new devices to learn, new recruits to train. Managing only the urgent issues is not enough.

That's why it's crucial to know your goal, to know your purpose, before you even start to make plans.

In an ideal world, you would spend 100% of your time on Quadrant 2 activities. Our world is not ideal, however, so I would suggest adhering as closely as possible to the 80/20 rule and trying to spend 80% of your time on the most important 20% of your tasks - the Quadrant 2 activities.

Let's see a real life example to explain the idea clearly.

I have a lot of urgent matters to take care of in my life. I have to pay bills. I have to be on time to the office. I have to solve immediate problems in my employer's database infrastructure. I have to buy groceries or prepared meals. But all of these activities are not that important to my true purpose. I could outsource most of them, if I had the resources. Often I find I have the choice to organize these things differently, as well (I can telecommute and do my job from home as efficiently as in the office).

A big part of my purpose is to be a writer. It's important to me, yet it's absolutely non-urgent. If I don't write, no disasters will occur. I will still be able to do my 9 to 5 job, to pay bills and buy groceries. I just won't get closer to fulfilling my purpose.

And that's why I make writing my top priority. I have over 40 daily habits, but writing is the most critical one. Every working day, I commit to writing at least 400 words and a minimum of 30 minutes.

Is it 11 p.m. and I still haven't written today? Even if I'm getting up for work the next day at 4:30 a.m., I stay awake and write until I achieve both of those metrics. Every day. Am I a superhuman? No, I do it because I know my priorities.

## Action Items

- Familiarize yourself with the important/urgent activity matrix.
- List all your regular activities and your goals and match them to a quadrant in the matrix.

# Don't Kill Your Time

*"Lost time is never found again"*
— **Benjamin Franklin**

One harsh reality the time journal will expose is the ways in which you waste time - your time killers. Every person has them. Mine were watching TV and playing computer games, reading popular novels, surfing Internet news and commenting on news articles just for the sake of commenting. I spent hours on those activities every day.

Do whatever it takes to convince yourself that time killers are keeping you from your life's purpose. Sitting in front of the computer or TV for hours rarely provides any lasting value to your life. This is time you could utilize in the pursuit of your personal mission.

One of the common regrets of people on their deathbed is, "I wish I didn't work so hard." Another is, "I wish that I had let myself be happier." But this doesn't mean people want to just hang out, wasting their time on meaningless or trivial matters. Is watching that sitcom making you happy? No, it just makes you feel good for the moment. It's a transient anesthetic.

Two out of the five most common regrets of dying people regard courage and busting out of your comfort zone. How much courage do you need to put your butt on the couch and turn on the TV?

The last common regret is: "I wish I had stayed in touch with my friends."

Notice it's not, "I wish I had played more Call of Duty with my friends," or "I wish I had watched more movies with my friends." Those activities are vehicles to spend time with your friends, not the goals themselves.

## Analyze How Your Spend Your Time

Pin down the time killers you use to feel better; activities which don't bring you closer to your purpose, but take up much of your time. Cut them ruthlessly from your life. As long as your yardstick is your purpose, it's relatively easy to root out these worthless activities. Just replace them with something worth doing, something truly fulfilling.

Killing time is suicide in installments.

I cannot word it any stronger. If you are not actively living, actively growing, you are dying.

I no longer play computer games.

I've read only two fiction books since October 2012. I severely limited my time spent wandering around the Internet and watching TV. These activities are simply not attractive to me anymore. I prefer writing, studying and spending quality time with my family instead.

## Action Items

- Make a list of your leisure activities.
- Measure the usefulness of each activity against the yardstick of your purpose. Next to those that advance your purpose, write how they contribute. Next to those that do not, write ELIMINATE.

# Work Every Day

*"I think and think for months and years. Ninety-nine times,
the conclusion is false. The hundredth time I am right."*

## — Albert Einstein

There is magic in consistency. I don't know the science behind it, but it's true. Getting back on track after holidays or sick leave is a struggle. Every Monday is a struggle, isn't it? Observe the mood at your office the next time you start a new work week.

Consistency is key, so work on your important projects as often as you can, preferably every day. Consistency builds momentum and continuity, while destroying inertia. It doesn't have to be a grand action each day. Do something small, but do it regularly.

I used to write only on workdays and take a break from writing on weekends. Getting back to the writing routine was always hard on Mondays. So I began writing every day, and in three weeks had been far more productive than my most productive month prior.

I set a guideline for myself to write at least 400 words each weekend. I overcame my obstacles. Busy Saturday? I just get up half an hour earlier.

I have a "no work on Sunday" rule. So on Sundays, my efforts are spent working on my novel or my personal blog. These activities are for my enjoyment, not for work.

Weekend writing led to an additional 15,000 words in 2013 and will accumulate into 40,000 more in 2014.

On workdays, I set an 800-word minimum, but I achieved an average of over 1,000 words per day during those 3 weeks - at least a 25% increase in productivity!

---

## Action Items

- Plan a daily discipline which will bring you closer to realizing your purpose; it doesn't have to be lofty, it just has to be consistent
- Practice it every day. Keep track of the time spent in your time journal.

---

# Break it Down

*"Very easy to understand; very straightforward.*
*But these are powerful and effective productivity techniques"*
## — Jim Rohn

The biggest threat to your productivity is your psychology. We are odd creatures. We are scared of our dreams, especially the big ones. When you look at an enormous task in front of you - writing a book, launching a website, establishing a business, preparing your kids to be effective, successful adults - it is easy to be immediately discouraged. It seems like so much work! How can one single man or woman accomplish it all?

In the case of tasks you have no choice about, like raising a child, you just somehow manage to achieve them. If you are like most people, you give up on tasks you "know" are just too big. You use excuses and procrastinate. The world will not end if you don't publish your book in this decade, will it? So you postpone it for an unspecified future.

This is **mental trickery**.

You are just as capable of starting a business or writing

a book as you are of raising a kid. You will need a different mental trick to overcome this fear - breaking huge tasks into a series of tiny ones.

Break the task down to the point where you will feel ridiculous if you avoid such a minor effort. If writing a book within two years feels like a challenge, then maybe writing one chapter a month is more reasonable?

Does it still look too big? Break it down further, decide to write 10 pages a week. Can you do it? If you think back to writing essays in high school and you feel it still surpasses your capability, break it down further: A page a day? A paragraph per writing session? A single sentence every hour?

Can you write one sentence each hour?

Sure you can. It's easy.

You have now out-tricked the mental trickery. It went from, "I can't write a book," to "It's easy to write a book."

Writing a book is a comfortable example. It's easy to imagine how to divide the writing process into smaller chunks. More complex tasks can be more problematic.

This brings us to another tip for breaking down tasks: write it down.

Let's take launching a new website, for example. Launching a website requires many tasks: domain name, hosting, specific technologies, design, graphics, multimedia, content, marketing, SEO ... Seems overwhelming, doesn't it? This is the mental trickery taking hold.

Take it out of your head and write it down. Marshall the points into chronological order. Take the first point and break it down into even smaller chunks (you must actually write it down). If you prefer to do this on a computer, trello.com offers a great project management tool that is free and easy to use.

## Example:

Domain name - what is required? Write it out:

- brainstorm ideas for the website's name
- research the availability of the best five
- comparison shop 5 domain providers
- buy domain from the best provider

Everything now appears simpler, more doable. Your mind is no longer occupied by appalling visions of a monstrous task; it focuses on small and manageable details.

As long as you keep your **vague and imprecise plans** in your head, your mind can play with them and make **bogeymen** out of them. **Write them down** and your ability to perform them will increase **tenfold**.

Writing down all the subtasks allows you to prioritize and serialize them, deciding what to do first, what to do next and so on. It also reveals the interdependencies between subtasks (e.g. choosing a specific technology may limit your hosting choices). All those steps will help you make better use of your time, but it's very hard to manage them all in your head. That's why they must be written down.

---

## Action Items

- Write down all your projects (or create a trello board).
- Break down bigger tasks into smaller chunks and repeat the process until each task is broken into its smallest subtasks.
- Prioritize and serialize the subtasks, taking note of interdependencies and tasks that have a specific order.

---

# Use a To-Do List

*"Rename your "To-Do" list to your "Opportunities" list.
Each day is a treasure chest filled with limitless opportunities;
take joy in checking many off your list."*

— **Steve Maraboli**

The dictionary definition of a to-do list is: a list of tasks that need to be completed, typically organized in order of priority.

The to-do list is the foundation of every time management system I've ever encountered. To organize your time, you need first to know what to do. Different systems offer different variations on this theme: daily, weekly, monthly, priority, job related, home related ... Your job is to work out which will be most effective for you.

I was initially attracted to the precise system of neatly organized groups as recommended in David Allen's *Getting Things Done* system. Unfortunately, it doesn't work very well for me; I have no central place to gather all the day-to-day obligations, what Allen calls the "inbox." I have labeled alarms on my company phone, company mailbox and private mailbox, as well as my notepad with ideas and projects, a spreadsheet with deadlines and two different software programs at work with ongoing tasks to take care of. It's hard to connect data from so many different input systems into one master list. It's doable, but managing this central system means additional work, which is not worth it.

Another possibility is to prepare your to-do list first thing in the morning, or for the next day before going to sleep. This also doesn't work for me. I'm unable to plan my day beforehand because it always seems as though some interruption comes up.

At first, this discouraged me. I tried several times to plan my day ahead of time. Then something would go astray and leave me feeling that I had wasted the time spent on planning the day before.

But even with my hectic schedule, I still use to-do lists. Again, keeping everything in your head is a losing proposition. My system is tailored to my life and may or may not work for you. Think about your daily schedule and habits and decide how to best use a to-do list in your life. Then, actually use it!

Today, I basically use two lists. The first is my daily habits list, which comprises about 30 habits. I've broken down some of the most important projects into daily chunks - working on my websites and blogs, networking through social media, reading, studying, writing.

I prioritize them; some are more important than others. For example, I can skip my workout or reading a blog post on my mentor's site if absolutely necessary, but I have to write and study the Bible every day.

I arrange the habit list, more or less, in the order of my day. My morning ritual habits - reading fragments of three different works, reviewing my vision board, repeating my personal mission statement and so on - are at the beginning. My "online" habits - visiting my friends' sites, following my mentors, working on my website and a few others - are in the middle. And in the evening, I work on habits like my gratitude diaries. I go through the list many times each day and check off the completed items.

I began using Coach.me to keep track of these habits at the end of September 2013, but before that I just used a paper notepad.

The other list I use is a simple set of items to be done that I keep in my pocket notepad. I always carry this notepad with me. This list contains the items which I don't do regularly, like ordering a book cover on Fiverr.com or paying the electricity bill.

As soon as I do an item, I cross it out. I don't prioritize or arrange the points on this list much. Some items are minor; some are major – but the importance of a task is clear as soon as I look at the list. I don't need any special ordering system to realize that buying my wife a gift for our wedding anniversary is more important than writing feedback for the software I decided to return a month ago.

I purge and rewrite this list about once a month, or whenever all the crossed-out points get too messy.

That's it, no rocket science. I will probably modify this system when I become self-employed, but for now, it serves me well.

Lay down your own system in a similar fashion, but don't copy someone else's approach verbatim. Read, study, borrow some hints and compose your own custom-made system. Just keep in mind that the most important factor is how you will implement it in your life. It may take some time to tweak it into a system that works with your life, but don't give up! A to-do list system that is truly compatible with your life is magic!

## Action Items

- Write down all of your typical tasks; cover all the areas of your life - your job, family obligations, obligations with your church or other organizations. Include your hobbies.

- Try different arrangements of those tasks to make a single list or a few of them; organize them by priority, where you need to do them, when you need to do them. Experiment until you find your ideal configuration.

# Block Your Time

*"Realize that now, in this moment of time, you are creating. You are creating your next moment. That is what's real."*

## — Sara Paddison

What does it mean to block your time? Blocking time is dedicating a specific period of time for a specific task. Guess where all this starts? Yep, it starts right in your head! We are back to the motivation factor again.

I've heard a lot of sound advice on this topic. Wake up earlier and do the job, find your "magic time" (when you are most productive) and reserve that for important tasks, use the Pomodoro technique, avoid distractions, check your email just twice a day. The list goes on and on.

My past choices have made me a slave to the agendas of others. I work as a database administrator, a job very similar to that of a fireman. Usually, I wait patiently for a disaster and when one comes along, I drop everything else at that moment and extinguish the fire (save the data). Often, this gives me long periods of time to do with what I please, but sometimes I honestly don't have five minutes to spare.

What about waking up early? I work on a shift system.

I live over 30 miles from my office. To get to work by 7, I need to wake up at 4:25 a.m. Well, I could go to sleep earlier and wake up even earlier, right? No, I have a wife and kids, and am dedicated to spending quality time with them. This makes it impossible for me to go to sleep before 9 p.m.

The shift system and family are very good at seizing my "magic time."

As for distractions, I need to have my work mailbox open at all times to respond to incoming alarms. The same goes for my Internet browser; several times a day, I need to use Google for work-related research.

But none of the factors above give me an excuse to not manage my time. I view them simply as realities that must be accounted for in my time management system.

I used to wake up 4:55 a.m. on weekdays, but now I get up 30 minutes earlier and use this time to ignite my day. I review my personal mission statement and vision board. I read fragments of two books which have shaped my philosophy. I read fragments of the philosophy manifesto I composed for myself. I sit at my kitchen table for 10 to 20 minutes to reflect on my life and state of mind. I write down these ruminations.

I decided that this is the best use of this 30 minutes. Those are the only ironclad minutes of focus, peace and quiet in my day.

I consciously check my Facebook account and private inbox only 2-3 times per day. I usually do it as a reward for completing other tasks, or as a way to relax for a few minutes. The same goes with reading news. I also force myself to check my sales on Amazon no more than once a day.

I try to block my time for writing. It is the first thing

I want to tackle every day. It takes quite a lot of time – anywhere from 40 minutes to two hours each day. I love to write on the train during my commute to and from work. I put earphones in and just concentrate on writing. On the train, there are no emails, no alarms, no people needing my attention. I said "I try to block my time" because the journey to work takes me about 60 minutes, so if I write longer than that, I'm forced to do it at work or at home. These are environments that tend to strain my focus.

Blocking your time also means is that you dedicate that time for only one specific purpose. So when I write, I write. When someone interrupts me - a coworker asking for help; my kids asking for dinner - I deal with the issue and then go back to writing. I don't try to juggle multiple tasks at a time. I do one task as long as necessary to finish the job for that day, then I go on to the next task in my queue.

There are many ideas on how to block your time, but they all come down to making you concentrate on one task at a time. One of the stranger bits of advice I've heard comes from entrepreneur Pat Flynn. He advises doing the dishes to put yourself into a work mindset. It is work, but it goes by quickly and is pretty mindless, meaning you can begin to mentally prepare for your next task.

Does this sound silly? Perhaps, but then again, Pat Flynn earns more than $500k a year. It doesn't cost anything to try this method, and maybe it will work for you, too. The idea is to research different techniques and try them for yourself, then stick with the solution most suitable for your unique situation.

All of the above advice has one thing in common: to do something, you need to give the work at hand your unwavering attention. You have control over your attention. Use it!

## Action Items

- Prioritize your to-do lists and block time for each task.
- Review and try the techniques mentioned in this chapter and pick the one that works best for you.

# Eat That Frog

*"Eat a live frog first thing in the morning and nothing worse will happen to you the rest of the day."*

— **Mark Twain**

D o you know why I deal with writing as soon as possible? Because it's daunting. Especially if I'm trying to meet a deadline. I admire reporters who produce article after article, day after day. If I'm excited about the subject, I write effortlessly. But I'm not always lucky enough to be writing about something that truly excites me.

So whatever task intimidates you most – do it first. Then, "nothing worse will happen." Every other job will be a cinch, in comparison. Completing the tough task first will give you a boost of productivity. You will feel like a winner, an achiever, and that will give you more energy to work on the next projects.

This tip drives to the core of human behavior. By **facing the hardest job first**, you are **building your willpower**, day by day. After only a short while, you will be invincible.

Many successful people, like Tim Ferris, teach that success comes from venturing out of your comfort zone.

In his book *The 4-Hour Workweek*, he gives the reader a challenge to simply lay down in the middle of a crowded public place for 10 seconds. The aim of that exercise is to get comfortable with the uncomfortable.

Train yourself in the habit of success. **Overcoming obstacles, excuses and fears is always a victory**. Facing the 'hard' task is really about overcoming fear, isn't it?

I try to organize my activities in order of difficulty. After a daily portion of writing, I go ahead with my "online" habits - I participate in online communities; I work on my website; I read my mentors' blogs; I comment. I don't like the mundane tasks on my websites - adding categories, editing the pages, including links, managing comments, installing plug-ins and so on. I find them boring, so I get them out of the way early. I love to read, so I leave the reading for the end of the day.

Don't stop with the first tough job. If you have a choice, pick another difficult, stressful or boring task from the list and conquer it next. Start your day strong and you will be more productive overall. You will feel better about yourself, which will bear fruits tomorrow, when you will face new challenges.

## Action Items
- Make a habit of taking on the hardest task first each day.
- Exercise stepping out of your comfort zone.

# The Sand Grains Method

"Who makes quick use of the moment
is a genius of prudence."

— **Johann Kaspar Lavater**

I developed this name for one of my fundamental time management strategies. Using the Sand Grains Method, you fill all your minutes with tiny tasks; these are the "Grains of Sand."

This approach is one of the core ideas in David Allen's *Getting Things Done* system. You put every single task on your list and then manage your time based on them. If you have a five-minute walk from the bus to the office, use that time to call a friend you've been meaning to call. If you are tired and need a break between job-related tasks, instead of surfing the Internet mindlessly, pick a task from your 'to do on the Internet' list: searching for a specific book on Amazon or reading that blog post you bookmarked a week ago.

Just as you can more efficiently fill a jar with sand than with stones, the sand grains method allows you to **increase your "productivity density."** I structure my habits around this idea. I have many activities which take 10 minutes or less. Speed reading practice, studying the Bible, doing pull-ups, reviewing my vision board, a High-Intensity Interval Training workout and adding my website to a web catalog all require 10 minutes at most.

It's really easy to fit several 10-minute blocks of time into your daily schedule. And that's exactly what I do.

The Sand Grains Method also helps in avoiding boredom and monotony. I jump from one task to another, and I feel the joy of achievement each time I cross out even a tiny activity from my daily plan. When my focus is strained from working on a long or complex task, I often feel the temptation to distract myself. I'm sure you are familiar with that urge to open Facebook or browse a news website. In such cases, I take one of the small tasks from my to-do list and complete it. This small accomplishment energizes me for further work on the bigger task.

Of course, not every type of activity is suitable for 10-minute blocks. I've been forced before to write in 10-minute installments, but I am much more productive if I write for 60-120 minutes at a time.

We are talking about fillers here, not your core activities. Believe it or not, even physical exercise can be a 'sand grain' activity. I don't plan long sessions on a treadmill or jogging outside. I just do a series of push-ups or other similar exercises here and there, a few times a day. For a white collar worker, it's enough to stay in shape.

Develop a plan for how to fill your schedule. Chop bigger tasks into smaller chunks and do them "in the meantime." If your job is to contact 100 people this month, divide it as described in the chapter Work Every Day, and send 3-4 emails a day. Composing and sending a single message, especially if using a template, takes mere minutes;

you can fit it in whenever you wish.

Each time you do a tiny job, you feel satisfaction from completing a task and it fuels your energy.

Always have something to do. I commute up to four hours every workday, and I see how people waste their time on buses and trains. I don't remember the last time I stared idly out of a train window. There are endless possibilities for filling that time! You can read, study, write, listen to a podcast, or do any combination thereof. Just be creative.

## Action Items

- Prepare a list of fillers in advance; don't spend your energy on wondering what to do next when you have a few minutes to spare.
- Break big tasks into smaller chunks, so you can do them "in the meantime."

# Multi-Tasking

*"There's never enough time to do all the nothing you want."*

— **Bill Watterson**

Multi-tasking gets a lot of bad press in the time management world. The common suggestion is to avoid it whenever possible. And rightfully so! I shudder each time I see my son doing homework and watching TV at the same time.

**But...**

You can do at least two things at once when one task is fairly mindless. Driving a car, doing the dishes, putting away laundry, cooking, cleaning - you do most of these jobs without straining your brain too much, don't you? What's more, you spend a lot of time on them. When I track all of my daily activities, I discover that I spend over two hours each day on such mundane tasks.

So use your mind while you are doing a purely physical job. Let me show you several examples from my own experience.

I listen to podcasts and audiobooks during my morning workout and while brushing my teeth.

I pray each time I walk to and from the train station or bus stop, and while doing household chores.

I've fallen in love with my Saturday multi-tasking. I listen to long hours of educational and motivational materials while vacuuming or scrubbing the toilet. I listen to them while running errands.

While getting to sleep and waking up, I pray and/or repeat my personal mission statement in my mind. It is soothing – I sleep like a baby and I start my day full of energy and enthusiasm, even though that day starts at 4:25 a.m.

It's your turn. What can you do mentally while in the cafeteria queue? While driving? While swimming or sitting in the sauna? During your commute or in the dentist's waiting room?

## Here Are Some Ideas

- Prayer: I read a lot of books written by saints, and they overwhelmingly agree that prayer and work are not exclusive. Most of them insist that prayer boosts one's earthly productivity.

- Visualization: To plan for success, you need a vision of a better tomorrow. You don't need special meditation sessions in a peaceful environment; using your imagination requires only your mind.

- Planning: This is similar to visualization; however, to plan something even as simple as a grocery list, it's very handy to have a pen and notepad at your disposal.

- Repeating affirmations or your mission statement: Here's another activity that only uses your mind. I'm skeptical of using too many affirmations. It's very hard for me to connect the dots, to find a relationship between something I say in my mind and a tangible result. Having said that, I have one or two that I repeat every day because they work for me. Another daily activity is repeating my 1,300-word personal mission statement.

- Self-analysis: Just converse with yourself, have a set of uncomfortable questions for yourself. I do it every day, with pen in hand, writing the answers down. Nevertheless, it's better to ask yourself constructive questions, without writing down the answers, than to let your mind wander idly while you do the dishes.

The mind is huge and the above examples are just a few of the boundless possibilities for mental-physical multitasking. One year at university, I got a summer job in a factory. I had to stand at the production line hour after hour doing manual labor. While I did this, however, I was also writing computer programs in my head. Be creative.

Another advantage of all these mental activities is that you are exerting control over your mind. Most of us are often unaware of what's going on in our minds. I was unaware for much of my life. Self-talk was something I took for granted. I no longer really listened to myself, I simply reacted, like in an old marriage or old friendship. I was with myself for so long that I was convinced I knew everything there was to know about me.

Often, self-talk is B.S., a projection of our fears and believed limitations. Les Brown presents this vividly: each time he had an aspiration, his other self would come up with obstacles and excuses:

"Who are you to achieve success? You don't even know your parents! You didn't go to college! You can't be a motivational speaker!"

By taking active control of your mental energies, you begin to strip your mind of these automatic, defeatist thoughts.

---

## Action Items

- Write down a list of physical activities you can use for multi-tasking.
- Schedule 15 minutes for brainstorming what you can put your mind into while doing the physical activities.
- Match at least one physical and one mental activity, and start practicing mental-physical multi-tasking.

---

# Conclusion

*"The time is always right to do what is right."*
— **Martin Luther King, Jr.**

Now you know the basics, go and implement them. The techniques I have shared with you are not rocket science, but they do require sustained effort. Start managing your time and never give up. I found I couldn't fully implement Dave Allen's *Getting Things Done* method, but just trying it gave me an incentive to seek strategies that better fit my life.

I've been amazed by my progress and productivity. I've transformed from employee (slave) into a blogger and writer who expects to be self-employed one day. You never know what you will unleash until you start!

Persevere.

Don't buy today's hype. Anything worthwhile takes time to develop. Don't expect to be managing a Fortune 500 company by next year.

Fine-tune your methods.

I deliberately avoided giving you an easy formula to follow. You have to explore this jigsaw puzzle and put it together in a way that will work for you.

I strongly recommend starting with the time journal first, but make your own decision as needed. Just pick one of the techniques I shared and start practicing it **today**. Develop your own disciplines along the way.

I would appreciate you sending me an email with news about your progress. I want to celebrate with you in your victories. Give me a peek into your story by sending a message to: **michal@expandbeyondyourself.com** or a tweet: (@StawickiMichal

Whatever your true purpose is – wherever your goals are pulling you – **I know that you have all the ability and the time needed to succeed on your path and beyond**. And I look forward to rejoicing with you when you experience success!

# FROM SHY
# To Hi

## Tame Social Anxiety,
## Meet New People
## and Build Self-Confidence

# Introduction

Shyness is a widespread problem. Our modern lifestyle fosters shyness over interaction. We are increasingly surrounded by machines and immersed in the online, impersonal world. For anyone living under the dark spell of shyness, it's a deep issue.

Shyness originates in the psyche, and though the pharmaceutical companies would like for you to believe that you can just pop a pill and banish your timidness, true change must come from within. Perhaps you have tried these pharmaceutical 'band-aids,' or perhaps, like most who suffer from shyness, you don't even consider it fixable. It's just part of your nature, right?

"I was just created that way," you say.

But shyness is curable. You were not born that way. Somewhere along the way, you nurtured shyness within yourself, possibly without knowing. Perhaps others labeled you as shy and you bought into that assessment. However it came about, you do have the power to reverse your timidness and find confidence in your dealings with others.

The shyness affliction comes in many shades, but if you are the type of loner who feels awkward while interacting with new people, and who avoids unknown social situations at all costs, then this book will help you – if you choose to allow it. Anxiety may be a part of your internal constitution right now, but people change. You can change, too. What is more, you can design your change. You can choose how far you take the process, and progress at a pace that is comfortable for you. You don't need to become a total badass overnight.

This book is designed to help you, a shy person, develop the regular practice of meeting and talking to strangers. People who are already confident in new social situations do not need my advice; they already know the benefits of this confidence. By practicing this discipline, you, too, will come to know the benefits as you expand your circle of interaction and influence.

First of all, talking to strangers will impact your internal world. Our actions determine our state of mind and our attitudes. Currently, part of your definition of yourself is, "I'm a shy person." Imagine how your life will change when you see an internal shift to, "I'm confident while dealing with other people."

Tiny changes in your behavior, in your interactions and relationships, will fuel big change.

> *"Dripping water hollows out stone,*
> *not through force but through persistence."*

The same goes with changing your attitude. Grandiose actions are not required. You do not need to give a speech to the masses tomorrow; you only need consistency.

The change in you will inspire changes in others. It's unavoidable. We are all connected. Your success and example will change others. Your success will lead you to new people and influence them. The lives of people you don't even know yet will be touched. Your influence will spread like ripples on a pond. I have seen it firsthand, and you will, too.

This change is enough to shake the world, and we don't have to start a political movement to drive this change. Collective change in many individuals is a powerful force, but collective change in many always springs from internal change in one.

Recall John Lennon's song, *Imagine.*

*"Imagine all the people,*
*sharing all the world ...*

*You may say I'm a dreamer,*
*but I'm not the only one.*
*I hope some day you'll join us,*
*and the world will live as one."*

That's the influence of one individual at work. It starts from a single person and spreads through society, changing the hearts of individuals one by one. All that's needed to realize John's vision is a change in a single human, and then the next and the next and the next, until "all the people" share similar values.

I don't preach any philosophy or religion. It's all about your personal impact on global society, an impact that is held back only by your clinging to shyness.

The influence and interaction game is an inside-out kind of thing. You can't impose on others what or how to think. But, you can share your opinion – not just with your words – but also (more importantly) through your deeds.

That's how it works.

People admired by society at large – Saint Teresa of Calcutta, Gandhi, Nelson Mandela, Martin Luther King Jr., Stephen R. Covey, to name a few – acted on that principle. They all were great influencers; people who left indelible marks on the progress of human society.

There are others who have different opinions. They prefer to manipulate, browbeat and deceive in order to influence people. They try to convince the world that their approach is quicker, easier and more effective. Many prominent politicians fall into this category.

At the core of every upheaval, there is a person who started it. Just one person. The world needs YOU, your unique voice and your interaction with other people, so you can influence your community, your country, our world.

This book is about gaining confidence by overcoming your shyness. It means building your mindset and attitudes through internal change, not by mastering tricks of manipulation. Manipulation and deceit will be unveiled in time; a change of mindset will serve you for a lifetime and have effects that ripple through our world long after you are gone.

You will find here my journey and my advice, but you are not obliged to conform to it. Your job is to pick up what will work for **you**, in your unique circumstances, and begin your own journey to self confidence.

# Confessions of a Shy Guy

I used to be quite shy. As an introvert, I've always been inclined to refer to my internal world first and refer to other people much later (if ever). It's not that I'm heartless; when I finally recognized others around me, I found I cared deeply for them. I realized I could relate to them. My heart sunk each time I saw people less fortunate than me. But, because of my conditioning, the times when I truly saw them were rare. And, when I did really see them, I found myself lacking the social skills to begin an interaction.

One vivid example says it all. Several years ago, I was heading home from work – a 30-mile commute. That day, I missed my train and had to wait almost an hour for the next one. On the same platform, probably waiting for the same train, were a young lady and her sick son. The boy was maybe three years old, about the same age as my own sons.

His bald head and frightfully thin frame told me he likely had cancer. Even the effort of raising a bottle of Coke to his lips caused his hand to tremble. He paused drinking to vomit in a plastic bag.

This young child was suffering like I have never suffered

in my life. His mother was caring, but firm. She held his head tightly when he vomited to avoid a resulting mess.

My heart dropped. I pitied them so much – mother and child both suffering so greatly there on that platform. I wanted deeply to talk to his mother, to offer her an encouraging word or a friendly chat to distract her temporarily. I wanted to tell the boy that I had two sons his age and that I thought they could become good friends ... but I couldn't. My own shyness prevented me from lifting another's spirits. I was unable to approach people I didn't know; unable to embrace the vulnerability required to reach out.

I actively talked myself out of trying to offer what I could to them:

"If you walked up to them, what would you say? That you are sorry for them? Words are cheap. And what have you to offer? Money? You are not rich. Time? You are a 9 to 5 slave. Encouragement? Can you cure the boy?"

I didn't speak to them that day; didn't express my compassion for them. If that had happened today, it would be a different story.

So, what changed? I changed.

Was it difficult? Yes, a bit. Was the change worthwhile? Absolutely.

Why do I tell you this story? Because we both know that being shy sucks, and this story, to me, best illustrates that. It's not my only example by any means, and they all left me with a sour taste in my mouth. I consider myself a Christian. I often felt my faith dictated that I try to offer comfort to others in hardship. For that reason, it stung even worse when I was unable to. I would like to say that this event shook me so hard that I was transformed from that moment on. It would have fit the stereotypes we worship – instant gratification, an easy fix.

In truth, I lived with my shyness several more years. I preferred hiding in my own world over reaching out to other people. It was uncomfortable. Human relationships were always a little puzzling to me. Social rituals always tired me. Diplomacy is not my strong suit. I usually say what I have on my mind. Often, it's not the thing people want to hear. I retreated to my internal world; it's my natural environment. I kept interaction limited to my closest family, a handful of friends, my brothers and sisters in my church community, and colleagues. I functioned that way for years.

I thought I could operate in that mode for the rest of my life. After all, I had my basic social needs satisfied. I didn't need strangers in my life; was indifferent to their existence. I recognized them only when I needed something from them: the shopkeeper in the grocery store, the guy on the full train occupying two seats, new colleagues in a new job – this was the limit of my social interactions.

Whether it was indifference or laziness is hard to say. I was relatively happy being in my small circle of relationships and my own mind. I associated every attempt to meet new people with unneeded effort, struggle and nuisance.

Shyness very often feels cozy. It allows you to shelter yourself in your own world without interacting with any of those 'odd' people around you. When you retreat, nobody can hurt you, right? But shyness is far from a blessing. Quite the opposite – in the long run, it's a self-imposed curse.

It's as true for you as it was for me. You don't need strangers in your life; you can live without them. But, allowing others into your life is required for growth. You grow only by embracing change, and there is no more unpredictable factor on this planet than another human being with his own free will, his own mind, his imagination and unique story.

In short – interaction with others is enriching.

Shyness is just one part of your internal construction, but you can rebuild yourself and overcome it. I know, because I transformed my own life. While still introverted, I consider myself outgoing rather than a retreating turtle. I still prefer my own company, but I'm no longer allergic to people I don't know.

A word of caution here – I'm not a 'regular' shy guy. I'm quite comfortable with public speaking, the biggest fear for most people. Training a group of new people at work or presenting to a class has never intimidated me very much.

I studied in two different cities, then moved twice for my career. In each of those cities, I was a member of a different church community. These communities relied quite heavily on speaking before the group. I was perfectly comfortable with that, partially because I immediately accepted them into my inner circle as my brothers in Christ, but also because I'm not generally afraid of public speaking.

One-on-one personal interactions with new people, however? Terrifying.

## There is Hope - My Transformation

When I decided to change my life, I decided also to confront the shyness that devoured any hope I had of connecting with others. In recognizing my renewed drive for growth, I saw how my shyness restricted me – an obstacle between me and the man I wanted to be. I also sensed that my behavior was flawed; it was against all my beliefs to be so reserved. I wanted to redeem myself. The memory of that trembling boy, weak and vomiting on the train platform was imprinted on my soul. My simultaneous desire and fear to reach out was an experience I didn't want to repeat ever again. Having deep reserves of compassion for the less-fortunate, but the inability to express them properly, wore on my heart.

When I set out to bring change to my life, I designed my daily disciplines around the principles given in Jeff Olson's *The Slight Edge*. One of the six habits I challenged myself to maintain from the very beginning was talking to strangers. I gritted my teeth, mobilized my willpower, and sought occasions to talk to new people every day.

I fell flat on my face.

I started too ambitiously for my timid, reserved personality. I was in no position to talk to strangers. The thought of approaching someone and opening my mouth paralyzed me. Each time I tried, my heart beat faster; my hands shook and butterflies raced in my stomach. Even thinking about those early experiences now causes my body to tense. Perhaps you know these feelings?

Talking to a stranger seemed to be the toughest, most impossible act in the universe.

But, I had my newfound sense of purpose; I was determined. With that attitude, I was able to force myself to talk with strangers a few times. I felt stunned after every successful attempt, but also exhausted.

I approached this like the average New Year's resolution. You grit your teeth and do the unpleasant new activity. It's not fun at all, but you feel like you achieved something, because you forced yourself to do it and overcame your limitations... And then, you fail a couple of times and decide that it's not such a big deal. You allow yourself a cheat day, a cheat week and before you know it, you're back where you began. And perhaps, worse off – if you then consider yourself a failure and beat yourself up, you are likely to subconsciously avoid any future attempts. You might continue to do your new activity randomly, when you feel like it. You lie to yourself and say that next week ... next month ... next quarter, you will get serious about it.

I faced this problem myself, but confronted it by habit-tracking. I started to track my disciplines. I used just a sheet of paper with the list of my habits-in-construction, each day ticking them off when I succeeded, or writing a minus sign when I failed. I tasked myself with talking to strangers every day.

Going through my notes after a few weeks, I realized that I had a lot more minuses in the 'talk to strangers' category than in all other habits put together. There was something wrong with my approach in that discipline. I examined my attempts, my results, and decided I was not ready to talk to strangers yet. Attempting it was draining my energy and undermining my self-confidence rather than driving growth.

This caused great internal anxiety. On one hand, I was all about transforming my life. On the other, I was already stumbling, and this was the first change I was attempting.

Habit-tracking allowed me to realize all of this consciously, kept it in my awareness. Habit tracking prevents you from pushing the habit back into the subconscious, where it will be deeply hidden – your brain's attempt to avoid unpleasant outcomes.

I realized that I was simply unable to talk to strangers on a daily basis – I was too afraid of it. It just wasn't as easy (or enjoyable, at the time) as studying the Bible for 10 minutes a day (another discipline I started). I had to change my approach.

Having this mental feedback, I could redesign my discipline. I painstakingly planned it from scratch. I'm a firm believer in consistency and continuity, so it remained on my list of daily actions.

But this time I started small. Because talking to strangers was too ambitious for me, I committed to just making eye contact with a stranger and smiling at him or her. I was so socially awkward that even this was challenging. Better, but I still collected some minuses in my tracking sheet.

I didn't want to stop at smiling, so I set three levels of difficulty.

Level 1: The relatively passive activity of making eye contact and smiling.

Level 2: Chip in on an existing conversation.

Level 3: "The hard level:" Start a conversation with a stranger.

I gave a lot of time and attention to details like this to rejuvenate the discipline. This was the key.

As Abraham Lincoln said:

> *"Give me six hours to chop down a tree*
> *and I will spend the first four sharpening the axe."*

# Shyness and the Road to Confidence

J im Rohn firmly believed that the etymology of a word
says a lot about the concept it represents. The word
"shy" derives from the Proto-Germanic *skeukh(w)az*,
which means "afraid." Many languages followed
suit: the late Old English *sceoh* – "timid, easily startled,"
the German *scheuchen* – "to scare away," the Old French
eschiver – "to shun," and the Italian *schivare* – "to avoid."

## Defining Shyness

Shyness is rooted in fear. Modern, psychological
definitions confirm this:

*"The primary defining characteristic of shyness is a largely ego-driven fear of what other people will think of a person's behavior, which results in the person becoming scared of doing or saying what he or she wants to, out of fear of negative reactions, criticism, rejection, and simply opting to avoid social situations instead."* —
Wikipedia

*"Shyness is the tendency to feel awkward, worried or tense during social encounters, especially with unfamiliar people. Severely shy people may have physical symptoms like blushing, sweating,*

*a pounding heart or upset stomach; negative feelings about themselves; worries about how others view them; and a tendency to withdraw from social interactions."*

— Encyclopedia of psychology

My stomach got upset just from reading that definition. It's so vivid and to the point. As is this one, from Free Dictionary's Medical Dictionary:

*"Brain activity is one component of shyness ... This may cause the person to blush, tense up, or start sweating. Those are some reactions caused when the brain signals its warning. The person may avoid eye contact, look down, become very quiet, or fumble over words."*

As you can see, shyness is fully connected with social encounters. It's an internal trait, but only influences you in social situations. It doesn't trouble you very much when you are alone.

Shyness defines, or rather constrains, your ability to interact with others, especially with strangers. When a shy person approaches an unfamiliar person, her brain starts to send its unpleasant and distracting warnings. It's hard to focus on social rituals and conversation when your heart is pounding so hard you're worried you'll have a stroke.

For me, it was upset stomach; the uneasiness of it near-indescribable, so strong as to almost be painful.

My hands would shake and my breathing would quicken. I couldn't gather my thoughts to say something relevant, let alone witty. Oh, and I had a lump in my throat. Why did none of the "expert" definitions mention this? Do you know how hard it is to say something coherently and confidently with a lump in the throat?! Yeah, good luck!

Each encounter was torturous.

Of course, there are varying degrees of shyness, varying symptoms, but it's never comfortable.

After each encounter, I suffered the sting of defeat. I would relive the experience in my imagination, pointing out every faux pas, every awkward line, and every time I could have given a better answer to a question. I beat myself up, called myself stupid, awkward and unsociable. I worried that every new person I met would immediately see these traits and label me. Each experience drove the painful spike of shyness deeper.

## The Roots of Confidence

The word confidence comes from the Latin *com* – "with," and *fidere* – "to trust." Modern definitions mildly convey this root meaning, but tend to skirt the core of it in our success-oriented society. Confidence now means:

- a feeling or belief that you can do something well or succeed at something
- a feeling or belief that someone or something is good or has the ability to succeed at something
- a feeling of self-assurance arising from an appreciation of one's own abilities or qualities
- a feeling of being certain that something will happen or that something is true
- faith or belief that one will act in a right, proper, or effective way
- a feeling that things will go well, but also a judgment on our own or others' abilities.

Confidence is a multidimensional concept, so it isn't used

much in psychology. Other terms are used to describe some of this: self-esteem (feelings about your self-worth), self-efficacy (feelings about your competence in relation to achievements, goals and life events) or optimism (the tendency to believe that one will generally experience good versus bad outcomes in life). They all focus on the internal meaning of confidence, not the part of the psyche that refers to judgments and beliefs about others.

Jim Rohn defines confidence a bit differently than psychologists, a definition derived from the etymology of the word. The meaning Rohn finds in the word confidence is much closer to the definition of confidence used in economics. Economists use a few metrics and terms related to confidence such as:

- Consumer Confidence - a measure of the level of optimism consumers have about the performance of the economy.

- Business Confidence - an economic indicator that measures the amount of optimism or pessimism that business managers feel about the prospects of their companies/ organizations.

These all stem from trust.

Rohn considered confidence one of the most elusive and misunderstood traits. It seems to be very self-centered, but he argued that "it is found to a greater degree in what we give to others than in what we have within or about ourselves." According to Rohn, "confidence has to do with inspiring trust," it's more of a social, than a personal trait.

Only when you feel trust can you act with trust. If you can state that you interact with new people trustingly, then you can freely state that you are a confident person and are no longer shy.

Confidence: you trust yourself to not be a jerk. You trust that the strangers you approach will be helpful, caring and supportive, rather than harmful.

You can build confidence. It's a character trait, and as such, it can be developed. I know it's hard to believe, especially if you are shy or if you've tried in the past and failed time after time.

In this way, you are similar to a little kid, who can't believe that he will learn to read one day. It seems overwhelming for that kiddo to acquire the skills and knowledge needed to master the art of reading. He needs to learn the letters, join them into words, build sentences out of them and comprehend their meaning. At the start, all these concepts are foreign.

But, nearly everybody is able to learn reading by following the educational systems developed over the centuries. The same goes with confidence. You may not be able to act confidently right now, but numerous people have developed confidence out of shyness and you are not so different from them.

Success comes from building confidence through new methods, a new perspective. Just ditch the old ideas; they weren't helpful in the past and won't be in the future.

The methods I describe in this book are not very different than the natural process of building confidence.

So, what are the natural sources of confidence?

First is your knowledge. You know that people are social creatures; it's normal for us to interact with each other. I assume you are not a psychopath, and you have some social bonds already established. Whether it's people in your family, at work or in your religious congregation, you were able to connect with other people.

You are intellectually aware of the fact that society is not seeking to harm or destroy you; 99.99 percent of the time, the worst thing that can happen to you from strangers is indifference.

Another source of confidence is the faith others have in you. If you were shy as a kid, I bet your parents encouraged you many times to attempt to play with other children. I do it all the time to my oldest son, who prefers playing on the computer over playing with his peers. When I encourage him to play with friends, it doesn't stem from my frustration about his social anxiety. Rather, it's the expression of my belief that he is perfectly capable of successful relationships; that he has the right to be confident in himself; that his own unique traits are not obstacles to connecting with others, but assets.

It's normal, natural, for people to cooperate. Every person that tries to interact with you – family member, friend, colleague or the person on the street asking you for directions – expresses the belief that you are a part of human race and, as such, are capable of social communication.

Your experience can also be a source of confidence. You are alive! That means you have already gathered the necessary life experience to interact with other people. No human is a lonely island. In fact, loneliness drives people crazy.

Confidence and shyness seem to be two poles of the same trait.

Confidence is the trust you put in yourself and, consequently, in others. Shyness is insecurity, a lack of trust in your abilities, fear you won't be socially accepted. You embody and communicate these feelings to others and in most cases you get what you give – not very satisfying interactions.

Every positive experience can reduce your shyness and boost your confidence. And, vice versa.

Anthony Robbins teaches about the feedback model, a model that perfectly expresses this concept. Your beliefs fuel your actions, your actions in turn fuel your experiences. Based on those experiences, your beliefs are shaped and the cycle begins once again.

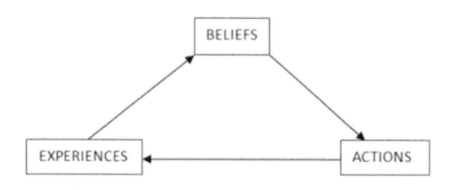

This can be a downward spiral, where your negative beliefs, fears and insecurities fuel shy actions. Those awkward attempts provide you with more experiences that 'prove' you are unworthy, a weirdo.

Those experiences further enforce your beliefs.

But when you add a new component into this cycle, a new quality, it can improve your life.

You can reverse the direction of that spiral. I offer you a full range of methods to do that, from the philosophy which shapes your beliefs to techniques that will add new actions and new experiences into your feedback cycle.

In conclusion: to build confidence, you need to work on trusting your abilities. But it's like the chicken-egg riddle – you don't really know which one comes first.

Trust is omnipresent in human interactions. You gained the existing trust you have in your traits thanks to your relatives, friends and other people with whom you've shared life experience. Your parents trusted that you were able to walk, talk and learn manners. Your teachers trusted that you could learn to read and write. Your friends trusted that you were cool enough to play with them. Those relationships made you who you are today.

Sadly, relationships can also be abusive and harmful and contribute to a lack of trust and confidence. But even these experiences need not define you today.

Talking to strangers is an ideal exercise to reduce your social anxiety and build your confidence. You will gain positive feedback information internally and externally. Your trust in yourself and others will fuel each other and grow simultaneously.

And it's easy.

## Where Does Trust Originate?

According to Stephen R. Covey, author of the bestseller *The 7 Habits of Highly Effective People*, trust is one of the basics of human society. Covey developed the concept of an 'emotional bank account,' which "is a metaphor that describes the amount of trust that's been built up in a relationship."

We need trust to act effectively. Imagine this situation: you are at a business conference and you are approached by a guy who wants to sell you on "a once-in-a-lifetime joint-venture business opportunity."

He gives a convincing presentation. He has everything in place. His business plan is flawless; his numbers are right.

But you don't know him.

Then, replace this guy with someone familiar. You've met him at several conferences in the past few years. You cooperated on a small project which was successful. He did you a favor or two. He introduced you to the CEO of a big company in your industry that he knew personally, and, as a result, your business saw a significant revenue boost. This person you know and trust gives you the same pitch.

How would you react to his proposal? Wouldn't you be eager to jump at this joint-venture opportunity of his? Where you might have responded with skepticism to the other guy, here you respond with excitement.

Trust is such an immaterial quality, but so basic and needed wherever interactions between people take place. That's why confidence, the quality which comes 'with trust,' is such an important factor in economic models. Trust is the fabric of human society. Business life is built from infinite numbers of human interactions. Trust in others is a foundation of success.

If you want to develop confidence, you need to work on trust. Conversations with strangers are a great way to achieve this. You gradually become convinced that people are not blood-lusting beasts. They are not an alien life form acting strangely or in ways dangerous to your well-being. As soon as you emerge unscathed from a few conversations, you begin to discover that people are just like you – they look for happiness; they have good and bad days; they have the same needs and fears as you. They are eager to talk about themselves, to share their experiences or just to socialize.

All of this makes deposit after deposit into your personal "trust account." Your feeling of safety with others will grow in general. It will affect your entire life perspective.

I largely got rid of my shyness. I sometimes still feel nervous in an unfamiliar social environment, especially when approaching beautiful women I don't know. But I learned to overcome those feelings and my internal world changed dramatically.

The biggest impact has been on my daily commute. I travel about four hours every day by train and bus; 90 percent of my interactions with strangers are while traveling to and from work.

I used to ignore the people around me. At best, I thought of them as a part of the environment. When I had a bad day, I perceived them as a threat.

Now I treat my traveling compatriots like a group of friends. I've already talked to dozens of them, and exchanged smiles with many more. I am no longer indifferent to them. I look forward to my daily commute with a pinch of positive anticipation every day: "Who will I meet?" An old friend? Someone outgoing? Someone overwhelmed with problems that I could encourage with a kind word? My commute has transformed from daily struggle to daily adventure.

# Indifference - The Core of Shyness

I don't know about you, but in my case, indifference was a big factor in my social anxiety. I had no occasion to gain trust through interactions with unfamiliar people, because I hadn't been interacting with them. By doing so, I was disassociating myself from a source of trust I could otherwise use.

## How Indifference Drives Shyness

The foremost reason for my indifference was complacency. I'm an introvert. I don't need many relationships to function. I'm quite happy being alone most of the time. I built several close relationships, but did not spread my net far. My family is my unrelenting source of support, soaking me with all the love and trust I need. In my mind, the price of being outgoing was just too high to bother.

So I stayed in my comfort zone. Sure, there were a few times of discomfort, like seeing the boy with cancer. But 99 percent of the time, I felt OK with myself, and I didn't need to spend any additional effort to achieve this.

Modern society strongly supports such attitudes. The number of personal relationships an ordinary person needs to function in society is the lowest in the history of this planet. In an era where you can order groceries, manage your bank account and send people gifts online, it's nearly possible to exist only interacting through technology. You can restrict the number of people in your tribe to the closest family, neighbors and colleagues.

There are people who have lived in their apartments for years and don't recognize their neighbors. There are people who work remotely, whose best approximation of work relationships is a Skype call. There are emigrants who see their families only a few weeks every year, if they see them that much.

New technologies support shrinking personal interactions. They make life easier, but they make it also less sociable. Take, for example, the virtual shopping cart – it is a vehicle of economic trust. You don't need to trust the guy with the small website very much as long as he is connected with ClickBank, which guarantees your money back if you are not satisfied with the product or service you receive.

The main goal of technology is to make life easier and perform daily tasks more efficiently. It does this job very well, but it robs you of the small opportunities to bond with others.

Technology has also stepped boldly into the world of entertainment. Video games, movies, television: all are amazingly effective in eating our time alive. I know something about this – I'm a computer game addict. Though I have largely curbed the problem, it is something that used to eat up a great deal of time that I could have used for more enriching pursuits. Even as an adult with my many occupations – father, husband, church community member and employee with a three to four-hour commute,

I was still able to play over 24 hours of Civilization IV in a month.

Games are everywhere. Mobile devices are more popular with each passing year, and now you can carry your own entertainment center with you. It is easier than ever to be distracted at any time day or night, at home or on the go.

You now have access to the whole world, but at the same time, the whole world also has access to you. It seems like everybody wants your attention: political parties vying for your vote; activist movements who want you to support their cause; charities who count on your generosity; and companies who want your money. If your firewall is not raised very high, if you haven't cut yourself off from these unwanted messages, you are exposed to a myriad of communication, and each one eats a piece of your attention and your time.

In effect, you have less time and attention for the people around you. All of those attention thieves make you more indifferent. These attention thieves alienate you further from strangers, makes them seem even further outside 'your tribe.' What is left of your time, you give to the close circle of people you know very well – usually your family and colleagues.

British anthropologist Robin Dunbar concluded that humans don't really treat other individuals as part of their race. According to him, we are only able to be close to a specific number of people. These people are a part of our 'tribe.' Called Dunbar's Number, he estimated it to be between 100 and 250. The rest of humanity outside this circle are unknown to us – inhuman.

Dunbar's conclusions have been readily accepted by the public at large. When I first heard of them, I was nodding in agreement. They seem to perfectly describe our reality. That's how our brains work: we really try to comprehend this complicated world of ours. In doing so, our brain filters and simplifies the billions of stimuli we get. As a result, we alienate people with whom we don't interact closely or often.

But is it possible to change that? Absolutely! You are the one who allowed time thieves and entertainment to hijack your attention. You can also reverse the process. The more I practice personal development, the more I believe that all we need to change are our attention and the uses of our time.

My Dunbar number was very low and I was consciously avoiding adding anyone else into my inner circle. But, daily practice and conscious effort to expand my comfort zone has changed this.

If shutting others out is so damaging and limiting to ourselves, why do we do it? Because you and I love ease. We are programmed to take an easy path. If you were to consciously process even 10 percent of the signals you get via your senses, you would collapse from information overload in no time. The brain tends to put everything not crucial to your survival in background mode. This includes your fellow human beings. It's so much easier to become indifferent than it is to sustain an extensive network of relationships. It's easier to touch your tablet or mobile phone than to touch another person.

Let's take, for example, the 'Like' feature on Facebook. It's very easy to click and make the other person aware that you saw her message and reacted positively to it. It's an order of magnitude easier than saying, "Thank you." in the comment section, or – God forbid! – explaining how the message made you feel or think.

We love ease of communication. But is it really easier to be dependent on those tools than to learn how to interact with people? You use them because, deep inside, you love to communicate. That's why social media sites are so popular. They made forming and maintaining relationships ridiculously easy. It's extremely comforting to use them. It is also alarming.

**394 likes and only 3 comments**

However, Jim Rohn states that the easiest things in life are the least profitable. I agree with him. It seems like everything that is easy and rewarding in the short term is difficult and unfulfilling in the long term. The opposite is also true. What is hard and unrewarding in the short term will become easy and fulfilling in the long term.

We don't pay attention to what's easy. In the long term, the use of these tools and systems leads to alienation. You will ignore people around you; your brain will put them in the background.

The real enemy of your transformation is not the companies who want your attention or the games which steal your time. The real enemy is you, because it's you who allowed them to do so. Without your cooperation, they wouldn't steal your time and attention.

This indifference to human relationships is crippling you. It's crippling our society. Stephen Covey wrote that low interpersonal trust increases the overall friction in any kind of cooperation. You focus on protecting your status quo instead of throwing yourself fully into the job at hand.

## What You Stand to Lose Through Shyness

Let's talk about a simple thing like asking for directions. If you are lost, it's obvious that locals can guide you quickly and effectively. One time, GPS guided me into the heart of a forest. I was looking for the highway. I stopped to ask for directions and the locals showed me a shortcut which I would never have found in the electronic database of GPS, a road to the backyard of a gas station near the highway.

The common opinion is that reluctance to ask for directions stems from a macho complex. I think it's just an uneasiness about talking to strangers.

Low confidence can cost you not only emotionally, but financially, too. There is a story in *Chicken Soup for the Soul* about a couple who wanted to attend a seminar in another state. Unfortunately, they had very little money. They called various people and institutions, asking for help until they got everything they needed – the plane tickets, seminar tickets, accommodations, meals and a rental car.

I've had similar experiences. My publishing career has been made possible because I asked for help. My English is mediocre at best. When I finished my first manuscript, I posted it on a Facebook community centered around personal growth, and asked for help. There, I found a noble soul who helped me edit my book. I can't imagine what would have happened if I didn't have that help; it's possible I would have quit then and there.

I made some connections in a Facebook authors' group and got the covers for all my books done for free. For my previous book, "Master Your Time in 10 Minutes a Day," my editor offered me free editing and marketing services. It made such a difference that my royalties were 15 times higher in February 2014 than in the previous month. To ask for a favor, you need some level of confidence and you have to overcome your shyness. If you won't initiate the interaction, nothing will happen.

You often need some level of existing 'Emotional Bank Account' deposits in advance, which means you have working relationships in place before you ask for help. For that, you need to be able to start and sustain relationships.

When I organized my time management book launch, I reached out and asked for help from fellow bloggers; 100 percent of those with whom I had prior relationships agreed to support me. Only 8 percent of those bloggers (two dozen or so) who didn't know me before gave me some real help.

Work on yourself in advance, before you need these relationships. You have to agree to a small level of discomfort to grow, to overcome your shyness and develop your confidence. The cost of avoiding strangers now may not seem very high – your social life is just a little poorer – but the opportunity cost may be huge. Develop your social skills before you really need them.

I preferred not to notice people around me and spent

my time in my internal world. I felt safer that way. However, it was a colossal mistake, because of my self-talk. Do you know who talks to you most often? You do. You and yourself have an endless conversation going in your head. It can be interrupted by external events, tasks or interactions, but as soon as you are left alone, you immediately go back to it. If you are like 95 percent of people, most of what you tell yourself is negative crap.

I was guilty as hell of it. I'm my own worst enemy. When I began my downward spiral of self-criticism, I used very rude vocabulary. I had no mercy on myself.

Unless you live in the most abject part of society, no one else is talking to you in more humiliating words than you are. I don't know any other human being who says worse things to me or about me than what I have in my own mind. I don't think I'm much different, in that regard, from others.

And you prefer this conversation over talking to strangers? You think that's more attractive than the "danger" of being vulnerable? That's a poor choice.

I've talked to dozens of strangers and the worst that happened to me was indifference. I buttonholed one man about the book he was reading and all he answered was, "Well, it's not very interesting." He just wasn't in the mood for a chat.

Compare that with my internal self-talk:

"C'mon, you jerk, talk to the guy! He won't bite you (I suppose)."

"Ha, ha, very funny. I know he won't bite me, you dunce, but what if he rejects me?"

"Oh, c'mon, don't be a weenie, talk to him!"

And then, after the stranger's answer, "You see, all my effort for no good! He didn't want to talk, booo!"

"And he was right, who would want to talk to such a loser?! Pshaw!"

All that the stranger expressed, in a very neutral way, was his unwillingness to chat, but at the same time, I experienced a whole lot of abuse from myself.

We tend to be very harsh toward ourselves. I wouldn't bear anybody else talking to me in such a way, but I do when it comes from within. Anytime I talk to strangers, I hear a majority of nice things. Their speech is always more civilized than my internal dialog.

I should certainly prefer their company over my own.

# The Mindset of a Confident Person

We tend to belittle the impact of right-thinking on our actions. We are all for, well ... action. I bet that since beginning this book you have been thinking, "All right, all right, but what do I have to do to be more confident?!"

## Your Mindset is Critical

Let's look at the definition of shyness once again:

"Shyness is the tendency to feel awkward, worried or tense during social encounters, especially with unfamiliar people. Severely shy people may have physical symptoms like blushing, sweating, a pounding heart or upset stomach; negative feelings about themselves; worries about how others view them; and a tendency to withdraw from social interactions."

Shyness (and confidence) starts in your head. The emotions are the bedrock, from which results physical symptoms, which then leads to action (or lack of action).

If you are a hardcore realist and dismiss affirmations and visualizations out of hand as woo-woo, it may be time to get real with yourself.

When I was researching self-talk for this book, guess what Google came up with most? The answer is one I wouldn't have guessed in a million years – sports performance. Where some focus on training methods and intervals, the equipment and other material factors, top performers focus on self-talk.

Our society is so deeply materialistic that we ignore the truth, we forget that everything we do starts in our heads. Scientists cannot measure everything in the human brain. They work hard and discover new things every day, but our knowledge of the brain remains the tip of the iceberg. We know how the atoms connect to create complicated chemical structures, but we don't really know how our brain works. It breeds a lot of confusion, and to avoid this confusion we choose to focus on the material side of things. We esteem "how" over "why."

Don't get me wrong. Action is great. It always wins over inaction. Doers always have an advantage over pure thinkers (or talkers). But, to act consistently over a long period of time, doers need some underlying philosophy that drives action. Having it, they don't overthink their actions. Even if they think too little, and are unprepared for obstacles, they reap the rewards of action by acting and failing forward. Without such a philosophy, they would fall into the cycle of giving up.

Mindset is crucial; it's a key to your success.

## Mental Exercises

To work on your mindset, you need mental exercises. They are great for the shy person, because they don't require them to actually go through the stress of approaching and talking to strangers. Start in your head.

Do you know the definition of madness? "Doing the same things over and over and expecting different results." You have to try something else if you want to progress, even if it feels woo-woo, illogical, or naive.

## Flex Those Muscles

What is the Muscle Testing Technique? Will I have to put on workout clothes and get sweaty? No. While the gym can be a great place to meet people, in this application, Muscle Testing Technique is just another name for using your imagination. Everyone has an imagination. Just like breathing, no one had to teach you how to do it; it is a natural, inborn ability all humans have.

The only problem I had with using this technique was that, at first, my imagination was so rusty that it was difficult to apply to overcoming my shyness. Once I realized that it was possible and I began applying it, it was a piece of cake.

Another obstacle you might come up against is the internal resistance to using 'new-agey' techniques. It's downright scary what kind of websites and mystical language spring up in Google when you search for "muscle testing technique."

I overcame my shyness because I was desperate to change my life. The skeptics had no answers for me. All they had to say was, "Live your life as it is and hope it doesn't get worse." Frankly, I couldn't pinpoint which of the more mystical or "new-agey" approaches helped me most. I simultaneously tried a LOT of different things. I was desperate to change my life – I was not looking to perform scientific research, giving each method a six-month trial and carefully plotting the results before switching to another. But even this unfocused approach helped me; I got the results I was looking for.

Don't be afraid of trying new things at the risk of feeling like an idiot afterward. Nobody sees you when you do this. After all, it's your imagination; it's in your head.

I also think that part of this resistance is just a subconscious inertia. Your brain loves the existing status quo and hates any changes. Using your imagination to solve problems seems like too much work. Your mind prefers to numb itself with a hefty dose of TV or video games.

Having said all of the above – simply using my imagination has helped me enormously and the results were almost instant.

The actual process is very simple. You don't need any special time or environment to do it. It won't hurt to have several minutes of peace and quiet, but it's not necessary.

Begin with visualizing the situation that causes you discomfort. As this book focuses on talking to strangers, I advise you to imagine yourself approaching someone you don't know. The more vividly you can see the details, the better. Therefore, imagine the specific person who you are shy around.

I should mention here that this technique is not really about visualizing the result. The sole reason for imagining yourself in this stressful situation is to elicit the uneasy feelings in your body – the butterflies in your stomach, a lump in your throat, etc. Any thought or picture in your mind which causes these physical reactions is good enough.

Once you are in this uneasy place, focus your attention, your mind, your awareness on it. There's no special technique here; you will know when you have mentally connected with your body's state.

Focus on these uneasy sensations in your body and

embrace them. They are part of you, the reactions of your own body. At first, don't try to have a dialog with these feelings or force them to change. Just be mindful of them; recognize them the same way you would recognize the sensation of a breeze on your skin.

Once you are aware of the sensations, ask your body: where do they come from? Why this tension? Why do I feel this way? Direct those questions at the unpleasant sensations, not to your body in general. You don't need to ask them all at once or in any specific order. They are just prompts for starting the conversation. Pick the question which most directly applies to your circumstances.

Once you begin the dialog, listen to your body's answers. Don't argue with them. Don't get mad at them. Just listen to them. Also, don't expect instant enlightenment. Simply start the dialog, something like:

You: "Why this tension?"

Body: "I'm afraid."

You: "What are you afraid of?"

Body: "I'm afraid of this person." (The answers come from your subconscious which is not the brightest part of your psyche.)

You: "Why are you afraid of her?"

Body: "Because she is attractive and I'm not."

Continue the dialog, and work it until you find the root of the problem. It's a left-brain activity driven by intuition, I can't guide you to your specific solution with hypothetical dialog. But to continue the example above, you could ask why you think you are unattractive or why the disparity in perceived attractiveness is holding you back.

Just keep listening. Your subconscious is quite dumb. It uses various excuses to stop you from getting into hot water. When revealed, the "reasons" may seem to be silly.

Silly or not, they are the reasons that keep you from talking to strangers.

Sometimes, such interrogation can lead you to your early life. You know, psychologists are not just a bunch of ignorant eggheads. There are genuine causes and conditions from your childhood that shape your adult behaviors. However, it is important to remember that these factors can be changed with sustained effort; they are not immutable.

The most important part of this process? Not to back off.

These images you call up, these sensations in your body, these answers you receive, are not likely to be pleasant. Going through them will cause you discomfort – this means you are doing it correctly. But facing them consciously makes all the difference.

You will stop reacting to those impulses and, instead, will interact with them. No longer will they drive you like lines of code drive a robot. You will suddenly find yourself with the ability to input your own pieces of code.

Once you start, don't stop. There is no single right way to do it right – there is only your way.

When I was introduced to this technique for the first time, it was a variant which didn't need words. There is a primal nature to it, more basic even than language. The crucial part of the Muscle Testing Technique is to call upon the images, sensations and thoughts you have when you try to approach a new person, and to embrace those thoughts, to replace your automatic impulses with conscious effort to understand what's going on.

I used the technique for the first time while doing my morning workout. I used a guided recording; the exercise itself took about five minutes, with roughly 10 more minutes of introductions and explanations.

At first, it all seemed a little bit "out there." The recording I used was about cooperating with your own fears. When the trainer asked me to visualize something I was afraid of, I thought about talking to strangers. At the time, all I could do was smile shyly at strangers. I didn't yet know how to overcome my fears and take these interactions to the next level.

But, thinking about the tension in my body ... how was that supposed to help me?

Despite my doubts, I did the exercises. I was a complete novice, but I repeated it the very same day while on a train to work. I remember I was sitting across from a lady I wanted to talk to. I came up with some compliment to start a conversation but, as usual, I was getting nervous.

I targeted the uneasy feeling in my stomach and embraced it in my mind. I don't remember if I chickened out that time, but I vividly remember the experience of consciously stopping the fear cycle and pondering it. For the first time, I wasn't simply reacting to the impulses in my subconscious mind and body, now I was now responding to them with my conscious mind.

That was my breakthrough moment. Regardless of whether I was actually able to begin a conversation in that moment, I was soon able to open my mouth and start meeting new people.

I'll repeat this to drive the point home: you don't need professional help to make this change; you don't need to practice it a lot; you don't need to do it exactly how I describe it or even believe that it works to get started.

Just. Do. It.

## Attention and Appreciation - Beating Indifference

Another way to practice your social skills without leaving your mind is the simple act of thinking about people around you. From time to time, turn off your internal dialog, take a look around and recognize others. Give them your attention and mental energy.

This is the first step in initiating a successful relationship. You can't approach other people if you are full of yourself and thinking only about your motives and needs. Such self-centered attitudes are the cornerstone of the shyness curse; they drive you to think mostly about yourself – "I am not good enough. I am such a failure. What will this person think or say about me... "

Indifference was a big part of my problem with talking to strangers. Dunbar's theory has merit; strangers are a bit like alien creatures. My imagination was making up impossible stories about them, just like a kid's imagination populating her wardrobe with monsters.

This exercise makes you more open toward other people. Remember what Jim Rohn said: you can't feel confident in yourself unless you put your confidence in others. To begin, you need to simply recognize their existence, and not just as part of your landscape. You must see the person as another human being with the same complicated world of thoughts and emotions boiling inside them.

So, who should you recognize? Everyone. Whether is it the "hot chick," the homeless guy, the old, obese lady or the man who looks like the CEO of a Fortune 500 company, you should give them the same attention. Essentially, we are all the same. We are hungry inside for attention and love.

Once again, it's not a bad idea to make this a meditation

exercise. Sit in isolation, close your eyes, relax, recall a few people you met that day and ponder them. The more attention, time and effort you put into your practices, the better the results.

The great thing about this exercise is that it is so amazingly flexible. You can do it in five seconds, while running to the bus stop. It works for everyone, even the busiest person in the midst of bustle or turmoil.

Small consistency always wins over massive but inconsistent action. I assume you believe you are simply too busy to spend half of your day on various mental exercises; however, building a habit of recognizing people around you will eventually show you that you do have the mental space to do just that. These exercises have a compound effect and will become second nature with practice.

You can practice anywhere – on a bus or train, while driving through traffic, in the mall, at work, or events, or while on a walk. Wherever there are people around you, you can exercise this part of your psyche. It's an ideal "filler" – an activity you can do while doing other, more physical tasks.

## Step One: Acknowledge People Around You

Stop thinking about your business for a moment. Look around you, find a person you don't know and give him or her a thought.

If you don't suspend your internal dialog, if you don't raise your head and take a look around, it won't happen. That's the minimal commitment you have to undertake.

## Step Two: Think About that Person

The bottom line is to think anything positive. When you have just a single moment, it's enough to stop and think about their image: "What a unique pattern on her nails," or "He has strong hands," or "This kid's cheeks are so cute," maybe "I like that jacket," or "What an interesting dress."

Your task is to get closer to the people, not alienate them further in your mind. Focus on finding in them something you can appreciate; something which will make them more human in your eyes. Two methods I have successfully used are to find the common denominator between us, or something I can appreciate about them.

Next time you notice the homeless guy and think: "Whoa! He smells worse than I do after an intense workout," you aren't improving the situation. Instead, confront that negativity and decide to think something like: "What hardship he endures every day; he must be a tough guy!"

The same goes for the other extreme, too. For example, if you see an attractive person and think, "Wow, I would do (insert sexual thought here) with him/her if I had the chance," you are dehumanizing that person. They become just a sexual object in your mind, not a fellow human being. When I see an attractive woman on a 5 a.m. train, I have trained myself to recognize her in admiration, rather than lust: "Wow, she put in a lot of effort to look her best so early in the day."

Be specific, impart them with human traits. Instead of thinking "Wow, that's one hot chick," think, "She seems to place a priority on taking care of herself."

As for the common denominator thing? Well, I simply try to find anything we have in common. If I notice someone with a kid, I immediately relate to them, because I'm a parent, too. When I see a rebellious teenager, I can relate to him, too; in my teens, I had long, greasy hair and a backpack with symbols and slogans scrawled in pen.

Because I'm a reader at my core, I can relate to anyone who reads, whether it's a magazine, an e-book or a paperback. The first thing I appreciate in every reader is their drive for self-improvement. Every kind of reading is valuable in my eyes.

If you struggle to find commonality with others, think of the subjects you are passionate about, the topics which are easy and natural for you. Write them down. Include them in your visualizations.

## Step Three: Praise Others in Your Mind

This is the natural extension of the previous steps. You noticed someone, you found what you appreciate in them and then you imagine starting the conversation with them by giving this praise.

From here, I find it easy to go beyond the visualization in my exercises. It's far easier to imagine myself saying, "I admire the loving patience you have for your kid. I'm a parent myself and I know what it takes," than saying "Excuse me lady, you have nice, slender legs." And it is easier to put it into practice later on.

This all may sound intimidating, but I assure you that after just a few days of practice, you will find yourself doing this instinctively. Each instance of the exercise will take you just a moment, but the results will be astounding!

## Visualizing Success

Another method of employing your imagination in developing your confidence is visualization. I'm someone who can hardly recall his mother's face in his mind. I'm sure my visualization skills are among the poorest on this planet. And yet, even I successfully used it on my quest to talk with strangers.

Because you are likely already better at visualization than I am, I will not give a comprehensive course in visualization here. I will teach you just the basics; the techniques I successfully used.

Again, you don't need a perfect meditation environment or 30 minute sessions to do it. Any place and time where your mind is free to think will do the trick, like while walking or working out.

At the core of the method I used – envisioning the conversation in my head, pretending that I am talking to a stranger. Imagine approaching someone and starting a conversation. If you have a vivid imagination and an 'avatar' – for example, someone from your neighborhood you would like to talk to, but feel too shy – then imagine that specific person. Visualization works better if you give your brain some convincing details. Just like a movie – if the acting is poor, it's hard to engage in the story. If the movie is good and the acting convincing, you are more inclined to believe it.

However, the key to visualization is emotion. The more positive emotions you foster, the more effective this exercise will be.

So, imagine that the stranger responds enthusiastically to your attempt to start a conversation. At your first words, he lights up and gives you a big smile. Imagine feeling at ease and enjoying the experience. Your visualization should include all the qualities you want to possess and express in your interactions with others – wit, confidence, firmness, sympathy – whatever it is that you pursue. Exchange a few sentences with the imaginary stranger, focusing on those qualities and trying to actually stir them up within yourself.

I recommend doing this exercise multiple times a day and always keeping it short, say under a minute. Do it while walking to the bus stop, in line at the cafeteria or while among strangers when you feel unable to start a conversation. Pick one person from the crowd and imagine initiating conversation with her.

This exercise has an additional advantage. Many times when you start it, your internal critic will turn on and try to meddle. That's what you want. It will allow you to get to know his arguments. As I said earlier, they are usually very weak. Once you hear what he is saying, you will be able to ridicule him, to shut his arguments down.

You can do this by altering the course of your imaginative conversation. For example, you say "Hi" to an attractive woman. Your internal critic chips in and the woman answers in the manner you are most afraid of – she screams: "Help me! This pervert is bothering me!"

Just by recognizing this vision, you realize how irrational this trepidation is. Then you can alter the situation asking with concern: "Where is he? I'll protect you from him!"

When my internal critic imposes on my visualization like that, I prefer to ridicule him using my imagination. So, in my mind, I add cartoon attributes to the woman's panic – her eyes get huge, her jaw drops on the floor and her long hair stands on end.

Using this technique, you transform a feeling of discomfort into a feeling of joy. The critic's job is to warn you and make you feel uneasy. He is a serious guy and has a hard time being ridiculed. He usually backs off for good after such a treatment.

I should mention, this is not my invention. This

technique is one of the elements used in Logotherapy, the psychotherapy school of thought created by Viktor Frankl.

Another advantage of visualization is that you exercise a conscious control over your mind and internal dialog. This is handy in just about everything. Every second you spend consciously is a second taken away from your autopilot, whose priorities are usually a bit different (typically: comfort, comfort and comfort at any price, here and now!).

I have personally found short, specific visualizations much easier than any advanced forms. As I mentioned before, my imagination isn't the best. Pictures in my mind are usually static, fuzzy and monochromatic. It takes a lot of effort for me to sustain any vivid image in my mind for more than five seconds. I cannot even envision my biggest dreams coming true!

But, this exercise is as much about the conversation as it is about images. The person I talk to is static, monochromatic and fuzzy, but the actual lines are clearly audible and the conversation flows uninterrupted. And I effortlessly stir up positive responses inside my mind and body.

These exercises work. If they don't directly build your confidence, at least they act as a vaccine against your internal critic.

# Hard Work Pays Off - Techniques for Conquering Shyness

I found a guide to the stages of conversation by doing a search online. I think it's an excellent summary of what's really happening during a normal chat.

1. Opening
2. Introduction
3. Find common ground
4. Keep it going
5. Wrap it up

But if you lack the confidence to start the conversation in the first place, such a blueprint is quite useless. You may know 40 excellent opening lines by heart, but if you don't have the courage to say any of them, they won't help you.

So, I modified the model slightly, according to my experiences:

## The 5 Stages of Conversation for the Chronically Shy

### 1.Opening

You need to muster your courage before you actually talk to a stranger. If I open my mouth, 80 percent of the job is already done. The rest is easy. When you are shy, the opening itself isn't a problem, because you simply don't open up. You don't approach the other person; you don't start the conversation.

Get yourself together and decide to start the conversation.

## 2. Introduction

Your first line may be important and lead the whole conversation to its final destination. Or, it may not. So don't put too much weight on it. You should mention some common experience or trait in your opening line, building the foundation for the next stage.

## 3. Find Common Ground

Ask questions. People love to talk about themselves or give their opinions. Look for what I call "a common denominator" – something you both share – a common characteristic, story, interest or experience.

## 4. Keep it going

Give your feedback or opinion about their remarks and ask more questions relevant to the topics already discussed.

## 5. Wrap it up

Finish the conversation with grace. Show appreciation by saying something like, "I really enjoyed our conversation." Or you can reflect back on the highlights to show that you were a good listener, such as, "Well, keep up the good work on your drawing project."

As you can see, I skipped the introductory stage. In my culture, it's not common to start the conversation with small talk and a personal introduction ("What lovely weather today, isn't it? I'm Michal"). When I gave it some thought, I realized that I have never introduced myself in a conversation with a stranger, but it has worked very well in my case. If it's common in your culture to introduce yourself at the beginning, then by all means do so.

## Preparing to Talk to Others - Passive Exercises

Let's talk about enormously helpful techniques that are accessible to nearly everyone. With the exception of people with certain actual handicaps, anyone can use these powerful strategies. Their usefulness lies in their passive nature. You don't need the cooperation of a stranger to use them. They all simply depend on your own actions.

This is an important quality for anyone paralyzed by shyness. In my experience, I was really afraid of interaction – what would the other person think or say about me? The truth is, they will always think and say something. You can't avoid that – it's at the core of interactions and relationships. Being paralyzed by such a thought is like sitting in your car and being paralyzed by thinking about how others drivers will react to your actions on the highway. It's just irrational.

### 1. Make eye contact

The advantages of making eye contact with strangers are twofold. First, you exercise control over your lack of confidence; you proactively diminish your shyness. Action conquers fears. You stop thinking about your imaginary limitations and start doing something. You don't need the cooperation of the stranger to make it happen. You have control over the process. It's you who chooses the particular person and when to do it.

The second advantage is that you start to learn that people around you are not mean or harmful. I used to populate the wardrobe of my mind with monsters who mocked or attacked me.

I've looked into the eyes of hundreds, maybe even thousands, of strangers during the past 18 months. Not once has the stranger attacked me physically. Not even once have I gotten an aggressive reaction. No one has asked me angrily, "Why are you staring at me?!" For that matter, no one has asked me that politely. Not. Even. Once.

Of course, I'm not talking about approaching the stranger and getting right in his face. All you need to do is just catch someone's glance. I make eye contact all the time, on public transportation, in church, walking down the street, at cultural events ... everywhere.

Eye contact is a tiny habit which will help you to introduce big changes in your life. It's how I restarted my quest of talking to strangers. I promised myself that I would look into the eyes of a stranger at least once a day. I felt I could do at least this much. It was so easy, I couldn't miss, and in that way, I developed consistency and didn't give up on overcoming my shyness.

The results? I'm no longer a shrinking violet.

## 2. Smile at a stranger

The next important step in becoming sociable is using your smile. Often we are so locked in our fears and insecurities regarding others that we don't notice they have their own struggles. Our fast-paced society isolates us, and the simple act of smiling can knock down the barriers between us.

So make eye contact and smile. You will be surprised by the mix of responses you get. Some people will flinch, wince or recoil: "A stranger smiling at me? This is so unexpected!" Many people will look away to break the eye contact, plainly feeling uncomfortable. Many will look at you incredulously: "Is it real? Is this person smiling at me?" They will take a quick look around for the person you are actually smiling at, before looking back at you when they realize they are the correct recipient of your smile.

The handful that smile back at me are the ones I love best. There will be such people in your case, too. But remember, if someone looks away or winces, it is reflective more of them than of you. Perhaps they, too, would benefit from this book.

So, how is this whole smiling thing done? Well, just look someone in the eyes and then force your mouth to twist into the resemblance of smile. That's not exactly the perfect way to do it, but that's how I started. You don't do anything perfectly at the beginning. In fact, when you start any venture you are in the lowest, least-experienced point. You will never do it worse than the first time. The only way to become better at it is through practice.

I developed the habit of smiling at strangers simultaneously with the habit of looking them in the eyes. A smile is the natural progression from a look. Do it at your pace. If you feel confident enough in this already, you can start with one of the more active techniques.

## 3. Step it up

If you are still afraid of talking to strangers, but you feel your progress is too slow for your taste, make the challenge bigger. I started with making eye contact with a stranger at least once a day, but quickly (within a week), I aimed for making eye contact with every stranger.

I went from forcing myself to smile, to making my

smile more natural. From there, I stepped it up again. I only considered the smiling exercise done when the stranger noticed me and my smile, and when he responded in some way, whether by flinching, looking away or smiling back at me.

Do the same thing over and over and over again, but do it more often and do it better.

## It's Go Time! - Talking to Others

These techniques build on your progress from the passive techniques. They are "active" because they require that you start talking to strangers. You will open your mouth and speak. Scary, right?

Well, not necessarily.

There are a few ways to make speaking to a stranger – finding the right words to use – easier. Definitely not foolproof, but easier. You can soften the "hardship" of talking to strangers using some of the simple techniques below.

### 1. Say "hi"

In my country, in my culture, it's uncommon to greet strangers. We just don't do that in Poland.

When my father emigrated to Ireland, he was thrilled by the fact that complete strangers would see him and greet him on the street. The simple act of kindness was so amazing to him. It was a major reason he decided to stay there permanently.

If it's socially acceptable in your culture to greet a stranger, then go ahead and do it. Like the other techniques, aim for once a day to start.

## 2. Chip in

Another way to overcome your shyness is by joining an existing conversation. You don't have to think hard over your opening line. You don't have to seek an opportunity to talk or get their attention. The occasion and the topic of conversation are delivered to you on a silver platter.

Let's say you commute to work by bus, and hear two people complaining about the bus being late for a second time this week ... excellent opportunity to pitch in.

Perhaps you are in the cafeteria queue and you hear people discussing yesterday's football match. It just so happens that you watched it, too, and are a fan of the same team ... you have an in.

Maybe you are at the electronics store and you stumble upon two guys wondering if it's better to buy an Android or an iPhone. You use one of those – chip in and share your experience.

These are mundane, everyday situations in which you find yourself without any hassle on your part. You don't need to take much initiative. This can reduce your apprehension or anxiety.

## 3. A common denominator

Another way to ease the entry into conversation is to find that you have something in common with a stranger, something you can easily relate to. I already provided examples of the subjects I felt comfortable with; the people I felt a little less nervous about approaching. I hope you used my advice and recognized yours, too.

It's easier to start a conversation if you have several such topics prepared beforehand. You can even prepare a set of opening lines. For example, I have some about reading:

"Do you enjoy that book?"

"Have you read more books from this author?"

"Would you recommend reading that book?"

"I've noticed your book has an interesting title – what's it about?"

"What genres do you like most?"

Such opening lines start the natural flow of conversation. I love to talk about reading, so once I begin, I have no trouble continuing the conversation. There is no threat of an awkward silence in the middle of the conversation.

## 4. Compliment them

Everybody likes to receive a compliment. I've never met with rejection when offering praise to a stranger. No one has ever told me, "Get lost!" after hearing my compliment. The range of reactions is wide and mixed, but it's always in the positive spectrum.

So praise away. Look at the stranger and think, what could you praise. Their style, clothes or a cool tattoo? Maybe some behavior you admire?

Starting the conversation with a compliment may not be as rewarding as talking about the meaning of life, but it's an order of magnitude easier. At the beginning, your goal is just to open your mouth and speak to the stranger.

All those mental exercises you did previously will come in handy now. You contemplated the strangers in your mind long enough to have some ideas of what you admire in others.

I'm a healthy, straight, male – meaning, I notice women. When I see a woman in the morning and notice her beauty, I appreciate the fact that she likely woke up an hour earlier than me to create this perfect look. In the evening, when

I feel half-dead, I appreciate a beautiful woman for her vitality. I appreciate small details they tend to apply to further enhance their look – like fancy earrings or colorful patterns on their nails. Their imagination seems to have no limits in that regard. I appreciate this, because I lack it. The greatest effort I can muster to look good is to shave my face and iron my shirt.

I appreciate all parents, especially loving and patient parents with many kids. I know what it takes. I appreciate all the readers in the world. As they say, "All leaders are readers." You can clearly see that commuting every day on a train. Many people are taking naps, chatting, playing with their phones or staring idly through the windows. Then there is that handful of people reading.

I appreciate those who are kind, polite and who show their concern toward other people. Those who smile back at me warm my heart. I'm always eager to start a conversation with them.

Do you see what's happening here? There is not an ounce of shyness in the sentences above – very few thoughts of myself, my clumsiness or vices.

This attitude makes you want to speak to strangers. The grain of confidence Jim Rohn talks about, the confidence in others, is already present in you if you face life with this attitude. Others sense your confidence, your sincerity, and they answer with the same. The process of communication flows effortlessly, as it should between two beings who are created to seek and share love.

Sometimes, you may find people are confused or apprehensive, unsure about your motives, when you compliment them. Let's face it, we are not accustomed to random praise from strangers, it's an unusual situation. So, don't expect a great spiritual experience or for someone to fall into your arms when you compliment them. Usually, they will thank you and that will be the end of the conversation.

And that's fine. This book is a guide to overcoming shyness and gaining confidence, not a textbook on how to have a rewarding conversation each time you approach another person.

But, you will have rewarding conversations too. Since starting this journey, I've had a few conversations that touched me so deeply to leave me with tears in my eyes, conversations that still move me to this day.

## 5. Step it up again

There is a danger of convincing yourself that small-talk is OK. But, we are working here on overcoming shyness and developing confidence. Don't stop at the beginning of your self-improvement road. If you feel like talking about trivial things or giving random compliments is not enough, you are no longer being challenged. It's time to take it to the next level.

You want to become good at bonding, trusting and relationships, not at gossiping. Don't go into a frenzy about it. You don't need to go to a bad neighborhood and provoke some hoodlums to prove yourself, just take your daily discipline to the next level.

If all you are able to do so far is say "Hi" to one stranger a day, try to do it twice a day. Or, add a compliment to your "Hi." Something like:

"Hi, nice haircut."

"Hi, I like your shoes."

"Hi, you have slender legs." (Just kidding!)

Whatever you are doing now, do it more, do it better. If you are already comfortable with praising strangers, try to add a follow-up to each encounter. Compliment their outfit and ask where they got it. Praise their tattoo and ask how they got the idea for it. Compliment their child and ask something about their family life.

Or, create a challenge by approaching the people you feel most uncomfortable around. For example, I always had difficulty talking to attractive women, so sometimes I forced myself to approach one and start a conversation.

By the way, a funny story about this: my wife just asked me what I'm writing about now. I told her I am writing about talking to strangers, then added jokingly:

"I'll write about how to talk to chicks."

"But you are not talking to chicks, are you?" she asked, with a note of dangerous concern in her voice.

"OK, I will teach them to talk to chicks and not to tell their wives about it," I answered with feigned exasperation.

My wife literally growled at that answer. I said, "Oh, I should record that sound and put the link in my book to emphasize the point!" ;)

Anyway, to take it to the next level, you must try something new, something which makes you uncomfortable. That's the fastest way to grow.

Don't overdo it. Take it one step at a time. If you fail a few times in a row at the more difficult discipline, fall back to the old plan. The worst thing you can do is to decide that you "just can't do it," and give up.

Consistency is the key. Do something every day, even if it's ridiculously easy for you.

# Analysis - The Key to Successs

Doing is enough, but analyzing your actions will boost your progress significantly. Therefore, analyze your progress, if not every attempt, then at least specific instances. Another successful strategy is to do an 'examination of conscience' at the end of each day.

## You, Under the Microscope

When doing this self-examination, keep your subconscious at bay. Your brain loves apathy and you are trying to stimulate it to work, so it's only natural that it will rebel. Remember who you are – a shrinking violet trying to grow, not some lounge lizard. Fears of being audacious or brazen are unfounded. If you notice such signs, it's likely that this is sabotage perpetrated by your subconscious: "See how you shocked this poor man with your big smile? Don't do that anymore or people will think that you are a freak!"

Don't be afraid of being too bold. I assure you, it's a vain anxiety.

I have practiced talking to strangers for over a year now and I still haven't banished all the old symptoms; boldness is still out of my reach.

The only thing you should be afraid of is the fear; it's what stops you from trying. You are a shy person and you have communication issues. Look for the signs of them.

You should analyze your failures, keeping in mind this definition: Failure is not doing the thing you intended to do. The only failure is not trying.

Anything else is a success. Even doing something wrong is a success – it gives you valuable feedback. But, planning to say "hi" to two strangers and not doing so is a failure and you should contemplate what caused it.

You should expect some failures, especially when attempting any new technique. Every time you try to do something new, you are the most vulnerable. You are out of your league. Like a baby learning how to walk, it's highly probable that you will fall down some. So expect the failures, but don't anticipate them. Don't dwell on all the things that could go wrong. As I already mentioned, if something goes wrong, there's a valuable opportunity to learn within that experience.

Self-analysis is just the last step in the process, which looks like this:

## 1. A plan or goal

What are you going to do? Make eye contact? Smile? Say "hi?" Start a conversation? How many times? Once a day? Twice? As many as you can?

What do you consider a positive outcome of the practice? A stranger will keep eye contact for a few seconds? Will smile back at you or say something nice to you?

As I explained before, I have three different levels – smiling, chipping into an existing conversation, and talking with a complete stranger. I consider the discipline a success when at least one person notices my smile and reacts in some way – looks at me incredulously, averts her eyes or smiles back at me.

It's important to set such reasonable goals. Sure, I have managed to start conversations with a few strangers that delved into topics as deep as life and death, but it doesn't mean I have to do this every time. My life is full of chores, tasks and activities, and I assume yours is similar in that regard. You can't spend all your energy and willpower on a single discipline at the expense of your other obligations.

Other benefits of reasonable goals: teaching your brain consistency and vaccinating yourself against discouragement – our subconscious mind's favorite weapon. You probably know this internal dialog all too well:

"Oh, heck I forgot to do my 40 squats today!"

"Crap! You are such a failure; you can't even do 40 squats a day. Don't bother with doing them tomorrow. What's the use?"

Setting small goals allows you to meet them every day and disarm your subconscious.

## 2. Tracking system

You need a tracking system to succeed. Your chances dramatically decrease if you don't track your efforts. 'System' is a big word, but it can be as simple as a pen and a pocket notepad. Too low-tech? Then track your progress on your mobile phone using an app like Lift.do. Whatever works for you is fine – just stick with it.

It has to be quick and easy to use. If your goal is to smile at 30 strangers a day, then try using a tally counter app on your phone. Every time you push a specific button, the app's counter increases its value. That way you can keep the device in one hand, smile, and track your efforts simultaneously.

On the other hand, if you just want to converse with one person a day, it's enough to open your journal at the end of the day and jot down "done" or "not done."

I'm quite good at tracking, because I track a lot of activities in my life – 40 to 50 a day. What's more, I've tracked my "talk to a stranger" discipline for well over a year, so I'm accustomed to keeping my tracking system in my head until the evening, and then writing down the results. Practice makes you a master. I don't bother to litter my memory with the exact number of people who noticed my smile. I just mark the fact that someone did when it happens for the first time each day. But, I don't let that fact absolve me from my goal of seeking opportunities to talk to strangers later on (or to smile at them through the day).

While I don't keep an exact count of smiles, I do mark the exact number of strangers I talk to per day, because it's a low number. In fact, I don't recall having more than three conversations with strangers a day. It's low, so it's easy to remember.

Track. It doesn't matter if you are in the mood or not. If the tracking itself is too absorbing, simplify. Don't complicate your life by introducing a complex tracking system. You should be able to record accomplishing your discipline as soon as it happens, and then come back to it when you have time for self-analysis.

## 3. Analyze

It's much easier to do self-analysis when you have data; that's what your tracking system is for. It is useless if you don't refer to it from time to time. You don't have to meditate or ruminate about your results every day, but it's not a bad idea. Consistency makes everything easier.

At a minimum, check every day if you've met your goal. As long as you have, you don't need to worry. Don't fix what's not broken. If you find yourself accomplishing your goals every day, it's time to think about taking the challenge up a level.

But, if you notice that you slacked off a few days in a row or regularly didn't meet your goals, that's the time for self-analysis. Again, don't listen to your subconscious too much. It wants to discourage you and get back to the "comfortable" status quo. It will happily use self-analysis for that purpose, if you let it.

Think rationally. Take a pen and paper, ask yourself questions, and write the answers down. Don't depend on your memory alone.

Some good questions for analysis:

- What happened? Why?
- How can I do it better next time?
- Was it too hard? Why?
- How can I make it easier next time?
- What did I think before and after the "failed" attempt?
- Did I forget? What kind of reminder could I use?
- Was I simply indifferent to strangers? What do I need to increase my commitment?

Analyze your emotions and the facts surrounding your attempts and design a new way around the obstacles you stumbled upon. Track your results and analyze whether the changes help. Just don't give up. That's the ultimate failure.

I recommend dedicating a couple of minutes every day, in the same place and time, to develop your habit. Do your self-analysis sessions in writing. When you don't accomplish your goal, try to work out the reason and a solution.

It's important to not only focus on the debacles. When you achieve what you planned for the day, don't dismiss the positive experience. Reinforce it. Thank yourself, or thank God. Recall the experience in your memory, relive it. Write your success down in your journal and how it made you feel. Or find your own way to reflect on and reward your success.

The takeaway is to enforce the good results by focusing on the positives. This is the moment to let your emotions run wild. Celebrate your success!

# The 21-Day Blueprint
# for Overcoming Shyness

I'm not a fan of 'success formulas.' I firmly believe, "to each his own." You have probably already noticed that the promises attached to most success formulas are ... well, just promises. What makes the formula successful is your implementation, not the formula itself.

## My Plan or Yours?

My story and my experience will always differ, in ways large or small, from yours. You need to read, absorb and synthesize my content to come up with your most effective solution. Having said that, I know that a lot of people love ready-to-use recipes for improving their life. They may lack the energy or resolve to figure out their own unique way, but be willing to try an out-of-the-box solution.

I already had one such recipe completed before I began writing this book. I wrote it for Lift.do a number of months ago.

I understand that not everybody enjoys jumping through various links while reading (myself included), so I made it a part of this book.

However, if you want to give it a shot, I recommend

joining this plan[1] on Coach.me. The application is free, and the social accountability it provides really helps make a better you.

Not ready to build your own plan? Try my 21-day Success Blueprint:

## The Blueprint: 21 Days to Success

### Day 1: The reason

Everything starts with a reason. If it's good enough, it will make you take continuous action. It doesn't have to be set in stone; your reason may evolve as you evolve, but you have to have a starting place. There are as many reasons as there are people, but you need to find your very own. In autumn 2012, I started my personal development program and overcoming shyness was just one aspect of it. I started this discipline to develop myself to a higher level. My progress is very important to me, so that was enough for me to start.

So why do you want to overcome your shyness? Why do you want to talk to strangers? Does it have to do with your past? Do you want to change your future? Is it going to help you at work or in your relationships? Examine yourself. Find your own reason. Write it down. Easy does it; it shouldn't be longer than a single sentence.

### Day 2: Notice other people

Start recognizing the people around you. Look at them and think about them. What things do you have in common? What things in them spark your interest? Write down a few of these.

---

1. http://coach.me/plans/254794/overcome-shyness-by-talking-to-strangers

## Day 3: Observe other people

Stop being lonely in your own mind. Look at the people around and think about them. What do their actions say? How they are behaving toward you? If you had to compliment one specific man or woman, what would you say? Write this down.

## Day 4: Eye contact

The first step in starting a conversation is to make eye contact. Stop avoiding other people's gaze. If you don't notice them, you won't talk to them. After successfully making and then breaking eye contact, give this person a minute of reflection. What things might you have in common? What things in them spark your interest? If you had to praise him/her, what would you say? Write these thoughts down.

## Day 5: Your internal voice

You are a shy person, right? There is some internal resistance in you which prevents you from acting casually in the presence of strangers. You have to unearth your self-talk, your habitual thoughts when you try to talk to a stranger. So go and try to talk to someone. Just like that. Browse around, choose one person, quickly think of a line to start the conversation. Start approaching the person. There can be only two outcomes: either you will start the conversation (congrats!), or you will talk yourself out of the idea. In that last case, I want you to listen carefully and remember what you are saying to yourself.

I was especially shy in approaching women. My thoughts were along the lines of: "What will she think of me? What if she freaks out: "Oh my god! Why are you talking to me, pervert?" Those are really irrational thoughts; your subconscious mind is not very brilliant. It's not the strength of these arguments which makes them effective, it's the negative feelings those thoughts trigger in your body.

If you have no experience in listening to your inner voice, I recommend a tool: Go to http://www. expandbeyondyourself.com/resources/reversingbelief. mp3 and you will receive an mp3 on self analysis. You may first want to listen to the Smart Passive Income podcast, episode 85, to hear some background on the development of this tool: http://www.smartpassiveincome.com/how-to-finally-take-action/

Listen to the recording and repeat the exercise on yourself. Imagine approaching a stranger: be mindful of the unpleasant sensations in your body and interview your inner voice. Once you recognize what you are saying to yourself, it's much easier to deal with it.

P.S. Don't forget to continue making eye contact with strangers several times a day.

## Day 6: Mental exercises

If you don't experience a breakthrough by analyzing your self-talk, you are probably still too shy to talk to strangers. That's fine, and perfectly normal. It took me several months to feel at ease talking to strangers (though I did not have the guidance that you have). Visualization can help you build this ease. Look at the people around you and think about them. Pick one person. Imagine approaching him or her and starting the conversation with some witty or engaging comment. Imagine that you are having a nice chat with the person. Finally, imagine that you are finishing your conversation and both of you feel at ease and enriched by the experience.

P.S. Don't forget to make eye contact with strangers several times a day. In fact, one of the people with whom you make eye contact may be part of your visualization. Reflect upon another person at least once a day.

## Day 7: Philosophy

You read it right – philosophy. You need an underlying motive to continually approach new people and talk to them. To do this, you must be genuinely interested in people. You can't think only about yourself and be good in interactions with others. They pick up on your attitude. You can't be motivated by a desire to "learn how to manipulate people and then rule the world" (insert ominous laughter here), it just doesn't work that way.

I think a lot of my problems in talking to strangers came from my experiences being involved in Multi-Level Marketing as a teenager. I approached people, focused on selling my idea, and that totally didn't work.

Everyone is unique and, therefore, needs his own philosophy. Some people are extroverts; they have the curiosity of a child and ask questions all the time. I don't think any of these people need this particular plan, but their underlying philosophy might be curiosity:

"I'm interested in people and their motives. That's why I talk to them."

My philosophy is the Christian philosophy – all people are my family. You need to find your own motivation. Your initial reason may not be enough to persevere in your commitment. Or maybe it will. Just ponder this from time to time, especially if you notice that you are slacking off in following this plan's guidelines.

P.S. Don't forget to make eye contact with a stranger several times a day. And practice visualization at least once a day.

### Day 8: Smiling

The next important step in becoming sociable is using your smile. Often we are so locked in our fears and insecurities regarding other people that we don't notice they have their own struggles. We all are so isolated in our fast-paced society, and the simple act of smiling can knock down barriers. So, make eye contact and smile. You will be surprised by the mix of responses you will get. Whether the recipient of your smile recoils, looks away or smiles back, there is profound power in a simple smile.
P.S. Visualize your interactions once a day. Make eye contact with strangers. Smile.

### Day 9: Practice

Visualize your interactions once a day. Make eye contact with strangers. Smile.

### Day 10: Practice

Visualize your interactions once a day. Make eye contact with strangers. Smile.

### Day 11: Practice

Visualize your interactions once a day. Make eye contact with strangers. Smile.

### Day 12: Practice

Visualize your interactions once a day. Make eye contact with strangers. Smile.

## Day 13: Practice

Visualize your interactions once a day. Make eye contact with strangers. Smile.

## Day 14: Practice

Visualize your interactions once a day. Make eye contact with strangers. Smile.

## Day 15: Practice

Visualize your interactions once a day. Make eye contact with strangers. Smile.

## Day 16: Compliment

A compliment is an easy way to start an interaction. Pick one person today and give them a compliment. Anything, really. Perhaps their outfit, their hair, they way they make room on the bus for the elderly lady. The "what" isn't important, but keep it appropriate. Remember, too, starting a conversation with a compliment is rarely as rewarding as talking about the meaning of life, but it's an order of magnitude easier. Your goal is to open your mouth and speak to the stranger. That's the best start.
P.S. Visualize your interactions once a day. Make eye contact with strangers. Smile.

## Day 17: Common denominator

Another easy way to open dialog is to find something in common with a stranger, something you can easily relate to. For example, I'm a reader and I LOVE to chat with other readers. I love to share reading experiences, to talk about books, authors, genres and styles. But I also spoke to strangers with smartphones when I was about to buy my first one. I'm comfortable with speaking to parents because, as a parent myself, I can relate to them. And so on. Think of the subjects you are passionate about, the topics which are easy and natural for you. Write them down; include them in your visualizations.

P.S. Visualize your interactions once a day. Make eye contact with strangers. Smile.

### Day 18: Ask a stranger about himself or herself

It's a little more advanced, but still an effective strategy. People are eager to talk about themselves. Almost everyone is hungry for attention. People love to talk about their experience, share their opinions and talk about themselves. The good communicator may use it to his advantage. Start the conversation with a question about the stranger. One of my favorite lines is: "I've noticed you reading a book. Are you enjoying it?" And then I have a set of follow-up questions: "Why or why not? Do you recommend the book? Have you read more works of that author?"

Such opening questions are a great start and you can go even deeper after you start the conversation. I once began to chat with a lady sitting next to me on a train with my "standard opening." She was reading a book about disabled children. Then, I asked whether her job was related to the subject and, oh boy, what a rewarding conversation ensued! "Be prepared," as the Boy Scouts say, you may receive much more than you expected.

P.S. Visualize your interactions once a day. Make eye contact with strangers. Smile.

### Day 19: Your first conversation

The exercises from the previous steps do work, I assure you.

But dry runs are good only up to a point. Today is that point. You can play it in your mind for hours, cooking up scenarios of conversations, but it won't substitute for the real experience. Today you must approach a stranger and start a conversation!

Well, if you're ready. If it really causes you great pain, practice your visualizations for one more week. And one more if you need it. Continue making eye contact and smiling. Every sustained action brings results. One day you WILL be ready to speak with a stranger. You don't have to do it exactly according to the plan; it must fit your needs. But ... the best way to overcome your fears is to face them. So why not face the challenge today? What is the worst that could happen by going through with it? Remember, the only failure is to not do what you set out to do.

P.S. Eye contact. Smiles. Visualizations.

## Day 20: Did you fail yesterday?

No?! You really did it?! Congratulations! Keep up the good work! Continue your commitment. Talk to a stranger today and tomorrow; keep the momentum going.

What if you did fail? Well, it doesn't matter! Your past does not equal your future. You've gained valuable experience and you are one step closer to your goal. Take 10 minutes today, get a pen and a sheet of paper and analyze what happened. Did you panic? Why? What thoughts were running through your mind? Did you talk yourself out of trying?

If necessary, go back to step 5 and repeat the exercise I recommend there. Whether you have succeeded or not, don't neglect your tiny disciplines. Visualize your interactions once a day. Make eye contact with strangers. Smile.

## Day 21: Rinse and repeat

You've reached the end of the plan, but your work is not done. Your goal wasn't just to talk to a stranger once in your life, was it? Rinse and repeat. Practice as long as necessary to make this habit automatic. For example, after a year of practice, I automatically seek to make eye contact with people around me. And whenever I look someone in the eyes, I smile. Talking to strangers shouldn't be something you need to achieve to prove yourself. It can be an activity which really adds value to your life and to the lives of the people you talk to. When you interact with others, miracles start happening!

## Looking Forward

Following the above 21-day plan is not mandatory. I even claim that it should be your last resort. It may give you an idea of what progress in overcoming shyness should look like, but I'm 100 percent sure you can come up with a better plan for your individual needs and abilities. After all, it's your life.

If you are a shy person, you probably have some painful memories and experiences. These experiences are yours in an intimate way that I cannot comprehend. You need your own ideas and your own tempo to win your battles.

Whether you use my blueprint or develop your own action plan, the most important thing is to get the desired result: in time, you WILL be able to talk to strangers. But you won't achieve this result if you don't start, or if you start and give up.

That's what The Ten-Minute Philosophy is for.

Embrace it and you will progress.

# Recommended Additional Lectures

- *The 7 Habits of Highly Effective People* by Stephen R. Covey
- *The Slight Edge* by Jeff Olson

# A Toast to the New Confident You

You need other people, you care about people, you are a part of society and you will not stop until you are sociable. Remember that you are your best cheerleader. You can't expect others to cheer you on, if you don't do it yourself.

Anchor this thought in your heart and mind:

**As long as you try, success is inevitable.**

The moment you stop trying, you've failed. But, remember that no reason is good enough to stop. Why resign if success is guaranteed? As long as you practice, you progress. Every day you try, you are closer to your goal. Sustained action always brings results. Don't defer it by giving your energy to doubts and hesitations.

When in doubt, keep a cool head. When moving forward, use your enthusiasm.

You will be unstoppable!

## New Friends, New Blessings
## The Gift of Giving

In February 2012, the millionaire Bernard Burchard launched a product, "Expert's Academy." He put some free videos on the Web to promote the launch. Bernard gave a challenge in his video — he would give away five tickets to his event and pay for the winners' plane tickets. The challenge: make a video talking about five life lessons.

I decided to try. It would be the first video I'd ever made. I wrote the script while commuting on the train. One of the points to cover was: "Take action."

As I worked on the script, I noticed an old lady sitting next to me deep in prayer. I thought: "I pray every day, we have something in common. I will ask her about her prayers." At this point, my shy part reacted with panic: "Oh, no! That would be rude! It will be disaster! Don't do it!"

And I didn't.

After several minutes, I wrote the words "Take action!" in the script. This time I felt compelled to speak to the old lady. I did, and found out that she had two very ill grandchildren, one with heart problems; the other, autism. I learned that their parents struggle financially. I decided to take action, and I've been helping them financially since that time.

The old lady's son-in-law is an atheist; he more or less makes fun of her Christian beliefs. The fact that some stranger is donating money for his son, solely because the stranger saw his mother-in-law praying, is incomprehensible to him. It's totally contrary to his worldview, where everybody cares only for themselves.

He didn't convert to Christianity or anything, but this gesture is a breach in his philosophy. Maybe, with time, it will transform into something greater.

That year, I got Christmas wishes from them. The lady I talked to, the grandmother of those ill kids, prays for me every day. And I get tears in my eyes every time I think about it (even now, as I write this).

That was the first time my chat with a stranger affected my life and the lives of others, but it's not the last. That conversation happened when I really did not feel ready to talk to strangers. It was a great struggle. But rewards that blossomed from it – being able to help others, knowing that I am making a difference – were well worth the struggle.

## Unecessary Intimidation

As I mentioned, I'm especially shy around attractive women. On my commutes to work (when most of my opportunities for meeting strangers occur), I spotted a woman about my age, who frequently traveled on the same train. Every day, we would get off the same train and walk to the same bus stop.

Many times, I came up with things to say to her, such as complimenting her outfit, but I never had had the courage to start the conversation. I was too intimidated.

I was transferred to another office, and this office had a different entrance. This time, we got off the bus at the same stop and began walking the same direction. Thanks to this, I realized that we worked for the same company; we had more in common than just the same commuting route.

One Friday, she had a heavy suitcase with her. I assumed she was leaving for a weekend trip right after work. I wanted to help her out and start the conversation, but I talked myself out of it. You know, the standard stuff: "What will she think of me? She looks like a strong, independent woman – what if she is offended by my offer of help?" And hence, I missed that opportunity.

The train's timetable changed and I changed rail carriers. I saw her less often.

Several months after the occurrence (or rather non-occurrence) with the suitcase, I noticed her on her way from a bus stop to the train station. I was reading on the bus, immersed in my book, so I was a little surprised to see her.

I was now months into my talking-to-strangers practice. I was more confident. I started a conversation, using the most mundane opening line in the world:

"So, you work for the same company as me, don't you?"

We talked a little about work, about commuting and about the disreputable city district we walked by on our route from the train to the bus. We parted at the train station.

She was a normal, nice person, and the long months of apprehension were caused solely by my internal perception of myself and the flawed opinions I had about her in my mind. I never would have known, had I not found a common denominator.

## True Depth

One day, traveling to work, I noticed that the lady sitting next to me was reading a book on an interesting subject – raising a disabled child. I started a conversation by asking about the book. She recommended it wholeheartedly. To keep the ball rolling, I asked her what her relationship was to disabled children.

She said she was a social or medical worker, I didn't dig for more details. Anyway, she worked with disabled children and their families on a daily basis. She told me how rewarding her job is. Some of her words: "pure love, simplicity, sincerity, no pretending, even ... mysticism."

I remarked how happy she seemed to have such a job.

She confirmed this after a second of reflection. It seemed to be a kind of revelation to her. We talked a little more about the lives of disabled people, their families. We talked about life, and about God. It was a truly enriching experience.

## Giving Inspiration

Another time on the train, a lady next to me was reading a paperback book in English. OK, a nice opening for me. I asked her how often she reads in English and where she gets the books. The conversation started to flow. Suddenly, she took charge, shooting a lot of questions my way: what do I do, do I have a blog, what is it about? It appeared that she was interested in personal development. She wrote down my blog address and name. I felt like I was giving my first interview.

I marked this conversation in my journal, because it was such a unique experience. That was on the 3rd of December, 2013. We met again on the train a few weeks later. We talked longer this time; we live in the same town and talked the whole way to work. I had recently gotten the hard copy of *The Slight Edge*, with my story featured in it and I shared that with her. She again was full of questions. I answered them as best as I could. I told her my transformation story and explained to her the Slight Edge philosophy upon which I built my Ten-Minute Philosophy. She was inspired enough to buy her own copy of the book.

We are friends now and we meet on the train as often as our schedules allow, about once every couple of weeks. I shared with Kamila the success of *Master Your Time in 10 Minutes a Day*. She was as shocked as I was by it.

Each time we talk, we discuss personal development,

philosophy and our future ventures. A week ago, Kamila confessed that she had started a few daily disciplines inspired by my example and the Slight Edge philosophy.

"I do 10 assisted push-ups every day," she said. "Until quite recently, I wasn't able to do a single one."

And how about that? An enriching friendship born out of a conversation with a stranger.

## A Quick, but Meaningful Moment

With time and practice, I became better at starting and carrying on conversations with strangers. I also became more confident. One day, I was on the train heading home from work. I hadn't talked to a stranger yet that day, so I was looking for the opportunity. I smiled at the lady sitting opposite me. She smiled back at me with a wide and sincere smile.

That's rare, at least in my country, on the 8 p.m. train, when everybody is going home after a long and (usually) tiring day at work. I estimate that only about one person in 20 smiles back at me on those evening trains.

"OK, level one checked off," I thought to myself. I stirred a reaction, so I accomplished the basic level of my discipline. I was done for the day. The train was approaching my town, so I got up, packed my laptop and put on my jacket. While doing this, another thought came: "What the heck? I should tell her that she has done something exceptional."

I sat down once again and said to her with a wide smile: "Do you realize how special you are?"

She was abashed. I could almost read her mind: "WTF?"

She answered hesitantly, "No, why?"

"You smiled back at me. I smile at many people, but not

many smile back at me. I think maybe one in 20. You are special."

"Well, thank you very much. It's what I do. I always smile back."

The anxiety left her. She was really touched by my remark. We had five minutes to talk about how people interact with each other. We had another common denominator – commuting – and we talked about that a little.

She thanked me a few times more for my remark. She said it made her day. It was a nice surprise for her at the end of the day. I started that conversation to appreciate her and I definitely succeeded. Two people felt better about themselves after this encounter.

## Shared Interests

Another time, I noticed a lady reading *Ender's Game* on a train. She was determined. There was quite a crowd; she had to stand the whole way. But, that wasn't stopping her from reading. I immediately felt a surge of sympathy for her.

I was sitting half a car away, writing. I wasn't determined to talk to her at first. I saw her about 25 miles away from my town, registered the fact in my mind and went back to writing.

But this was an instance where preparation bears fruit. I had trained myself to notice people around me, so I noticed her. We both exited the train at my stop, the last station on the line. I caught up with her after getting off, and started the conversation:

"Hi, am I mistaken or did I see you reading *Ender's Game?*"

She nodded in assent. I asked her why she picked this title and the conversation started to flow. And, oh boy! It was the one of the best 'reading' conversations in my life. I accompanied her for a half mile or so, not exactly in the direction of my home.

We talked about our favorite books and authors, about genres we like and meaningful reading experiences. She was the soul mate of the reading part of my personality.

I utterly enjoyed that conversation; it was like talking with an old buddy. I hope to meet her again on the train and continue our conversation.

## Confidence and Building a Business

Confidence is an amazing trait that helps you act with greater determination and focus. Like most authors, when I started writing, I fell victim to the impostor syndrome. I didn't feel worthy of teaching other people or sharing my experience.

Objectively speaking, I was a failure. I let complacency take over the better part of me. I was doing just enough to get by in my job, marriage, church and every other area of my life. I wasn't confident at all.

But, in life, everything affects everything else... The more I published, the more open I was, my results in talking to strangers improved. The better I was in talking to strangers, the better I got taking big, bold action in my writing ventures. I started my mailing list, joined several Facebook groups for indie authors, and began my official writer's blog.

Preparing my previous book launch, my marketing adviser recommended that I contact other bloggers and ask them for support. I felt extremely uneasy doing so, but I overcame my fears and reached out. People who knew me beforehand helped me without a moment of hesitation, but I was surprised to get some help from people who I didn't know at all. The book launch was an amazing success.

I discovered that getting to know people online is similar to getting to know them offline. While only a few of the bloggers I contacted were able to help me on the launch, I was enriched by every interaction with them.

I suffer from the impostor syndrome quite a lot: "I'm not a self-help guru. I didn't achieve much." The feedback trickling back from my readers is dismantling this attitude bit by bit, but I still experience trepidation when shouting my message out to the world.

While writing this book, I had my weekly Skype call with my accountability partner. It was the second week in a row that I failed to contact other bloggers asking them for help in promoting my Ten-Minute Philosophy. I confessed that it had more to do with my insecurities than with the actual lack of time. He said that this was an ideal case to show my readers this book. I hate when he is so right.

I mustered the courage and reached out again to my acquaintances. And again, I received support well beyond my expectations. They shared their success stories, some of them expressed interest in establishing a long term partnership, and some of them shared my idea with their followers. I overcame my anxiety and I touched the lives of people I would never have without this act of boldness.

Now, go out into the world. Make your own success stories! I want to hear about them!

## Jeanne:

If you need a "first person" to talk to, you should try
talking to the clerk that rings up your groceries or your fuel
purchase. Usually people that hold these jobs are "talkers"
like I am.

## Liz:

Realize that nobody really pays attention to you if you say
something silly/off – it doesn't matter. Such realization is
liberating.

If you stay away from the crowd, people think you
are "stuck up" or conceited when they first meet you. If
that idea horrifies you, that's cool – it's a great incentive to
change.

Talk to chatty people. They are happy to have someone
listen to them and they do most of the work. When you are
finally comfortable (and perhaps bored), it is easier to make
conversation with others.

Party survival tip: pick out someone at a party who
looks more miserable/shy than you and cheer them up.

## Peggy:

I don't think so much about criticism from others, because
I find 99 percent of people seem to either welcome the
exchange or are indifferent and prefer to keep it short.

# My Free Gift to You

Thanks for reading all the way to the end. If you made it this far, you must have liked it! I really appreciate having people all over the world take interest in the thoughts, ideas, research, and words that I share in my books.

I appreciate it so much that I invite you to visit my site:

**www.michalzone.com**

... where you can register to receive all of my future releases absolutely free.

You won't receive any annoying emails or product offers or anything distasteful by being subscribed to my mailing list. This is purely an invite to receive my future book releases for free as a way of saying thanks to you for taking a sincere interest in my work.

Once again, that's **www.michalzone.com**

# More Books by Michal Stawicki

*A Personal Mission Statement: Your Road Map to Happiness*

*Trickle Down Mindset:*
*The Missing Element In Your Personal Success*

*The Art of Persistence: Stop Quitting, Ignore Shiny*
*Objects and Climb Your Way to Success*

*99 Perseverance Success Stories: Encouragement for Success in*
*Every Walk of Life* (with Jeannie Ingraham)

*99 Habit Success Stories: Proven Successful Habits of Everyday*
*People, Authors, Entrepreneurs, Celebrities and Prominent*
*Historic Figures* (with Jeannie Ingraham)

*Power up Your Self-Talk: 6 Simple Habits*
*to Stop Beating Yourself Up and Reclaim Your Life*

*Get Rich Quotes for Every Day of the Year*
*from The Science of Getting Rich*


**Six Simple Steps to Success series:**

Vol. 1 [free]: *Simplify Your Pursuit of Success*

Vol. 2: *Know Yourself Like Your Success Depends on It*

Vol. 3: *Bulletproof Health and Fitness*

Vol. 4: *Making Business Connections that Count*

Vol. 5: *Directed By Purpose*

# A Small Favor

I want to ask a favor of you. If you have found value in this book, please take a moment and share your opinion with the world. Just let me know what you learned and how it affected you in a positive way.

Your reviews help me to positively change the lives of others.

**Thank you!**

# About the Author

I'm Michal Stawicki and I live in Poland, Europe. I've been married for over 20 years and am the father of two boys and one girl. I worked full time in the IT industry before becoming an author. My passions are transparency, integrity, and progress.

In August 2012, I read a book called *The Slight Edge* by Jeff Olson.

It took me a whole month to start implementing ideas from this book. That led me to reading numerous other books on personal development, some effective, some not so much. I took a look at myself and decided this was one person who could surely use some development.

In November of 2012, I created my personal mission statement. I consider that the real starting point of my progress. Over several months' time, I applied numerous self-help concepts and started building inspiring results: I lost some weight, greatly increased my savings, built new skills, and got rid of bad habits while developing better ones.

In the next several years, I published 17 books, started a book advertising business, downsized my day job to quarter-time, and liberated my wife from her day job.

I'm very pragmatic, a "down-to-earth" person. I favor utilitarian, bottom-line results over pure artistry. Despite the ridiculous language, however, I found there is value in the "hokey-pokey visualization" stuff and I now see it as my mission to share what I have learned.

My books are not abstract.

I avoid going mystical as much as possible. I don't believe that pure theory is what we need in order to change our lives; the Internet age has proven this quite clearly.

**What you will find in my books:**

- detailed techniques and methods describing how you can improve your skills and drive results in specific areas of your life
- real life examples
- personal stories

So, whether you are completely new to personal development or have been crazy about the Law of Attraction for years, if you are looking for concrete strategies, you will find them in my books. My writing shows that I am a relatable, ordinary guy and not some ivory-tower guru.

Printed in Great Britain
by Amazon

67181842R00169